POLICY AND PRACTICE IN HEALTH AND SOCIAL CARE

NUMBER SIX

*Health and Social Care:
Establishing a Joint Future?*

POLICY AND PRACTICE IN HEALTH AND SOCIAL CARE

POLICY AND PRACTICE IN HEALTH AND SOCIAL CARE
SERIES EDITORS
JOYCE CAVAYE and ALISON PETCH

Health and Social Care: Establishing a Joint Future?

Alison Petch

Director
research in practice *for adults*
Dartington Hall Trust

DUNEDIN ACADEMIC PRESS
EDINBURGH

Published by
Dunedin Academic Press Ltd
Hudson House
8 Albany Street
Edinburgh EH1 3QB
Scotland

ISBN: 978-1-903765-73-9
ISSN: 1750-1407

British Library Cataloguing in Publication data
A catalogue record for this book is available from the British Library

Typeset by Makar Publishing Production
Printed and bound in Great Britain by Cpod, Trowbridge, Wiltshire

Contents

Series Editors' Introduction

Partnership working has become a central feature of New Labour's modernisation agenda for health and social care. Partnership working is no longer recommended as good practice; it has become a requirement.

Developing a partnership approach can be challenging, however, with commitment to collaboration varying widely across agencies and between the different professionals involved. In practice, partnerships can range from sophisticated models designed to sustain long-term delivery of services to examples of tokenism, more concerned with being seen to collaborate than with genuine attempts at integration. Partnership working has provided a focus for a broad literature which offers a range of theoretical frameworks with which to understand partnerships, their shape, structure and potential outcomes, and the processes involved. It has promoted a new vocabulary of collaboration, co-operation, integration and joint working.

This volume acknowledges the distinctive approach to partnership working adopted in Scotland under the auspices of the Joint Future Agenda. Using a case study approach, the author traces the evolution of the Joint Future Agenda within the broader context of partnership working in the UK. She examines the areas initially targeted for partnership working and tracks the progress made. Drawing on her own experience of evaluating health and social care partnerships, she explores the extent to which policy and practice are rooted in an evidence base and questions whether joint working is delivering the outcomes valued by service users. The result is a theoretically informed and empirically supported critical analysis of partnership working. It provides an excellent baseline against which to compare other joint working and integrated service initiatives

Dr Joyce Cavaye
Faculty of Health and Social Care,
The Open University in Scotland,
Edinburgh

Professor Alison Petch
Director, **research in practice for**
adults*, Dartington Hall Trust,*
Totnes, Devon

Acknowledgements

I would like to take this opportunity to thank my former colleagues at Glasgow University, Ailsa Cook, Emma Miller and Ailsa Stewart, for their invaluable contributions to our many debates on the intricacies of partnership working. My thanks also to Ann Rosengard, Peter Gunnell, Chris Taylor and Isla Laing who conducted the case studies cited in Chapter Three. I would also like to acknowledge the prompts to my thinking of Caroline Glendinning and Bob Hudson through their seminal papers on the theme of partnership working.

The quotations prefacing each chapter are from the study 'Users and Carers Define Effective Partnerships in Health and Social Care' (Petch et al., 2007).

Glossary of Abbreviations

ADL	Activities of Daily Living
CDSET	Carer Defined Service Evaluation Tool
CHP	Community Health Partnership
COSLA	Convention of Scottish Local Authorities
CPA	Care Programme Approach
CSCI	Commission for Social Care Inspection
DHSS	Department of Health and Social Security
ELPA	Extended Local Partnership Agreement
ESH	Education, Social Service and Health (Pathfinder theme)
JFIAG	Joint Future Implementation and Advisory Group
JIT	Joint Improvement Team
JPIAF	Joint Performance Information and Assessment Framework
LHCC	Local Health Care Co-operative
LIT	Local Improvement Target
LPA	Local Partnership Agreement
OT	Occupational Therapist
PCT	Primary Care Trust
PIP	Partnership in Practice agreement
RUM	Resource Use Measure
SSA	Single Shared Assessment
SSA-IoRN	Single Shared Assessment Indicator of Relative Need
SSP	Strategic Service Partnership
SWSI	Social Work Services Inspectorate
UDSET	User Defined Service Evaluation Tool

CHAPTER 1

Mapping the Territory of Health and Social Care Partnerships

*If your health suffers, your social suffers, and if your social
suffers, your health suffers. So it's better to be all working
together if you know what I mean.*

The volumes in this series explore the extent to which, for each of the featured areas, there has been a distinctive approach in Scotland compared with other parts of the United Kingdom. This discussion of partnership working across health and social care has the benefit of a specific initiative in Scotland, with a programme of linked developments which can act as the centrepiece for the comparison. The volume has three main objectives: to inject an element of clarity into the multitude of debates as to the nature of partnership working; to examine the extent to which there is an evidence base to support partnership working; and to explore the emergence of the Joint Future Agenda in Scotland.

The scope of this volume

Partnership working has featured as a constant theme in both national and local policy over the last decade and more, and has been a strong feature of the policy documents produced by 'New Labour' since 1997. Potential partnerships have been promoted across a range of statutory and independent agencies, and at different levels of formality. Health and social care has been a particular focus for partnership working, with increasing emphasis on collaboration for both policy and practice agendas. Moreover, partnership working between health and social care is of particular interest to this policy series because there have been significant differences in policy development between Scotland and the rest of the UK.

A key feature in Scotland has been the development and implementation of the Joint Future Agenda and this offers a valuable case study of partnership working. It will provide the basis for an exploration of how partnership working is conceptualised and the extent to which policy and practice is rooted in an evidence base. Exploration of the Joint Future Agenda will touch on a wide range of issues pertinent to health and social care. These include the nature of the assessment process, the ways in which central policy is translated into frontline practice, the extent of local variation, and the extent to which partnership working needs to be mandated or can be achieved on a voluntary basis.

This initial chapter will seek to distil clear definitions from the somewhat confusing literature in which partnership working and related terms are often used to denote a range of different types of relationships between agencies. It will explore the rationale behind the promotion of partnership working, define the dimensions for partnership working, and evaluate the extent to which partnership working is supported by an evidence base.

The concept of partnership

Partnership working may initially present as a relatively straightforward concept. It conjures the idea of two or more agencies (or teams, or individuals) working together for some assumed common purpose or to achieve a shared objective. Yet very quickly a proliferation of related terms emerges: collaboration; co-operation; joint working; co-location; co-ordination; inter- or multi-professional working; inter-agency working; multidisciplinary working; integration. Writing and debate is bedevilled by the use of different terminology – and by the use of similar terms to mean different things. The Audit Commission (1998) concluded that it is a 'slippery concept', while Ling (2000, p. 82) portrayed 'methodological anarchy and definitional chaos'. One common thread is a tendency to use the term 'integration' once the parties have combined into a single agency. Under this formulation partnership can be considered as the process and integration as the outcome. This also reflects the reality of a continuum of partnership working: tentative collaboration between specific individuals at one end of the spectrum, through formalised joint delivery, to combination into a single agency, full integration, at the other. Partnership working therefore becomes an umbrella term for all degrees of inter-agency working short of merger.

Liddle and Gelsthorpe (1994) suggested a useful hierarchical classification which identified five levels:

- Communicating partnership – agencies recognise that they have a role to play in relation to each other but do not take this beyond communicating.
- Co-operating partnership – agencies agree to work on a mutually defined problem, but maintain separate boundaries and identities.
- Co-ordinating partnership – agencies work together in a systematic way and may pool resources to tackle mutually agreed problems.
- Federation – agencies operate integrated services, sharing some central focus.

- Merger – agencies become indistinguishable from each other working on a mutually defined problem and they form a collective resource pool.

Miller and Ahmad (2000), for example, identify what they consider to be the defining characteristics of inter-agency working, of inter-professional collaboration, and of partnership working. The latter, they agree, is the most inclusive of the formulations. They acknowledge, however, that 'the very flexibility of the term creates problems in establishing whether or not an appropriate partnership, or one that embraces all legitimate stakeholders, is in place or knowing the nature of such a partnership' (p. 13). As important as the specific definition that is adopted, is the need for clarity and precision as to the concept of partnership being used in any debate: lack of clarity and precision is likely to lead to both confusion and contradiction.

While this wrestle with definition may be frustrating for those simply concerned to map and make sense of the territory, it may serve a more useful purpose for those concerned to promote an appearance of consensus. Clarke and Glendinning (2002, p. 33) have characterised this position:

> Partnership has the advantage – in terms of political rhetoric, at least – of being relatively non-specific. While this lack of specificity may be a source of concern to policy analysts, it has some distinctive political benefits. Like 'community', partnership is a word of obvious virtue (what sensible person would choose conflict over collaboration?). It is unspecific about the dimensions, axes or composition of particular 'partnerships'; partnerships can exist between sectors, between organisations, between government departments, between central and local government, between local government and local communities, and between state and citizen (at least). Despite their wide variations in organisational and social relationships, processes and arrangements, partnerships provide a key, overarching and unifying imagery of this Third Way approach to governing.

As prefaced above, a key dimension in any discussion of partnership is 'who are the partnerships between?' Is the debate around partnerships between organisations, and if so, at what level? Partnerships may be strategic; they may operate at the front line; or they may be focused at the intermediate level of the team. The relevant organisations may be statutory agencies – as in the current consideration of health and social care partnerships – or they may embrace private or not-for-profit elements of the independent sector. They may be at a local, regional or national level. Alternatively, partnerships may be between stakeholders, for example between different professional groups or between professionals and service users. Hudson (2002) suggests that inter-professional partnerships have received less attention in the debate, but where they have featured, doubts have been raised as to the feasibility of effective joint working. From his own study of general practitioners, social workers and community nurses in three localities in the north of England he presents a more positive picture. Three key areas are identified: professional identity, professional status, and professional discretion and accountability.

In their review of effective partnership working, the Audit Commission (1998) associates the use of the term 'partnership' with six key features of a joint working arrangement. According to their definition, a partnership links partners who are otherwise independent bodies but agree to co-operate to achieve a common goal (1). A new organisational structure or process is created to achieve this goal (2), planning and implementing a jointly agreed programme (3), often with joint staff or resources (4). Relevant information is shared (5), and risks and rewards are pooled (6).

The rationale for partnership working

The arguments for partnership working in its various forms are often taken for granted. It is assumed that some form of collaboration will lead to more coherent and effective service delivery. There will be opportunities, as argued by Beresford and Trevillion (1995), for added value and benefit from individuals and agencies working together, with the potential for new insights and solutions. The process of partnership working allows enhanced understanding of the roles and rationale of other professionals and offers the opportunity both to understand other working cultures and to create a new, shared culture. There is often the assumption that partnership working will lead to a range of efficiencies: less duplication of effort and therefore a reduction in valuable staff time; shared information and therefore a reduction in lead-in times; a broader understanding both of an individual's situation and of the wider resource environment and therefore a more appropriate service response. The assumption of cost savings is a logical conclusion to such efficiencies.

An element of caution is introduced, however, by Beresford and Trevillion (1995). They suggest that the divergence between different professional and organisational interests and cultures may be underplayed in the drive to bring partners together and that the needs of more vulnerable groups or communities may be ignored or excluded. The design and implementation of new structures may become an end in itself, distracting attention from the core business of delivering support. Moreover, even when structures are in place, the development of systems and procedures may become an end in itself, a further diversion that leads to a loss of direction. Ovretveit *et al.* (1997) offer a comprehensive discussion of the theoretical principles of partnership working and in particular of the perceived advantages and disadvantages associated with different models of team working. Potential models have been widely debated, for example by Molyneaux (2001).

Three different rationales for partnership working were identified by Mackintosh (1992) and are frequently cited. The first focuses on 'synergy' or added value, the product of partnership working being greater than would be achieved by the parties working on their own. The second model refers to 'transformation', seeking change in both the aims and cultures of the partner organisations. Finally, the 'budget enlargement' model indicates partnership working motivated by the desire to gain access to additional funds.

The Audit Commission (1998) considers that there are five main drivers behind agencies pursuing partnership working. These are delivering co-ordinated packages of service to individuals; tackling the so-called 'wicked issues', challenges that cross traditional organisational boundaries; reducing the impact of organisational fragmentation and minimising the impact of any perverse incentives; bidding for or gaining access to new resources; and meeting a statutory requirement. The Commission recognises, however, that this prescription can be difficult to achieve: 'partnership working is difficult to do well and making partnerships work effectively is one of the toughest challenges facing public sector managers' (p. 5).

Newman (2001, p. 109) has suggested that a number of objectives may drive partnerships and joint working. These can include:

- 'to create an integrated, holistic approach to the development and delivery of public policy;
- to overcome departmental barriers and the problems of 'silo' management;
- to reduce the transaction costs resulting from overlapping policies and initiatives through coordination and integration;
- to deliver better policy outcomes by eliciting the contribution of multiple players at central, regional, local and community tiers of governance;
- to improve coordination and integration of service delivery among providers;
- to develop new, innovative approaches to policy development or service provision by bringing together the contributions and expertise of different partners; and
- to increase the financial resources available for investment by developing partnerships and joint ventures between the public, private and not for profit sectors.'

A more theoretical approach to partnership working advanced at an early stage by Hudson (1987) continues to have relevance. He suggests that organisation theory can offer models for understanding partnerships in health and social care. In particular he identifies three main components: environmental context; organisational network; and collaborative linkages (the degree of formalisation, of intensity, of reciprocity, and of standardisation). In terms of environmental context, external factors may act as incentives for partnership working, particularly where there is a 'turbulent' field. Indicators of turbulence include a field containing a large number of organisations, an inability of agencies to satisfy the demand for services, the introduction of new programmes or legislation, and a retrenching economy. Change may be difficult, however, in a turbulent environment, with organisations seeking to remain in control in their field or domain. An organisation may be asked to invest scarce resources and energy in developing and maintaining relationships when returns on this investment may often be unclear or intangible.

The dimensions of partnership working

A case study by Hudson *et al.* (1997) of working across primary health care and social care boundaries in five localities developed what they termed a 'collaborative continuum' to describe the primary care/social care interface. This was based on two key dimensions: the degree of integration and the degree of trust. Four distinct points were isolated on the continuum from lower to higher levels of trust and integration. At the lowest level was 'isolation/encounter', followed by 'communication', then 'collaboration' and, at the highest level, 'integration'. Of particular interest from this study is the identification of ten key themes, described as the 'juxtaposition of alternatives' – choices and options which often characterise partnership working initiatives. These juxtapositions offer a useful context for the discussion within this volume.

The first juxtaposition identified is *organisational shift versus individual entrepreneurialism* as the catalyst for change. This debate focuses on the extent to which developments depend on champions for change (reticulists) who will secure progress despite traditional bureaucratic and hierarchical systems. Hudson and his colleagues suggested three important dimensions in respect of champions. Firstly, they may emerge – individuals with drive and enthusiasm who are able to garner political and organisational support. Alternatively, champions may be appointed (witness the recent enthusiasm for 'czars'), possibly continuing work already laid down by earlier leaders. Champions may also, it was found, disappear, a weakness of any strategy that depends upon individuals rather than more formal agreements.

The second juxtaposition is *excellence versus equity*. Where resources are scarce, should the focus be on those already favourable towards partnership working – and what then is the impact in terms of equity? *Costs versus benefits* highlights the need to consider the trade-off between the investment in promoting partnership working and the activities that could otherwise have been pursued with the same resources. The juxtaposition of *medical/ nursing versus social models* captures the potential clash in culture and values between different professional groups, while *flexibility versus agreements* introduces the extent to which arrangements should be formalised.

The decision as to the management model to adopt for partnerships is raised in *project management versus mainstream management* and the physical location for partnership working in *co-location versus non co-location*. A key juxtaposition in any move towards integrated working is the potential tension between *team loyalty versus organisational loyalty*; this may also be reflected, as in the case study in discussion of role identity, in *social work versus care management*. The final juxtaposition derived from this study is *markets versus hierarchies versus networks*. This reflects a common presentation of different models for co-ordination; in the case study of primary health care and social care the dominant model in those more advanced on the continuum was shown to be the more informal structure of networks. Aspects of these juxtapositions will recur throughout this exploration of partnership working.

A range of commentators have reflected on the barriers which challenge partnership working. Professional ideologies and cultural identities are a common feature, explored in detail by Dalley (1989). There may, for example, be distinct professional beliefs around the role of institutional care or on the 'duty of care'. She identifies the distinct behaviours and attitudes which grant professional identity but which can also lead to defensive tribalism and a promotion of tribal ties at the expense of looking outward. Pietroni (1996) has presented an account of the stereotypes associated with different professional groups. The doctor is the hero-warrior-god – 'fighting the disease', administering 'the magic bullet'; the nurse is perceived as the great mother 'angel of mercy'; while the social worker's lot is often to be portrayed as the scapegoat. These authors have also shown that even student professionals in each group already characterise other groups through stereotype. While at one level these are amusing, they can emerge as more serious barriers to collaboration.

A variety of strategies to overcome the range of barriers to partnership working have been proposed over the years. These can be distinguished according to the key driver. *Co-operative* strategies, for example, work on the basis of mutual agreements. *Incentive* strategies offer some form of carrot, for example a greater resource allocation, whether in money or in kind, while under *authoritative* strategies agencies or teams can be instructed to work together. As with the juxtapositions above, these different strategies should be kept in mind in the context of the Joint Future Agenda case study.

There have been a variety of attempts to identify the conditions for successful partnership working. Building on the three components identified above (environmental context, organisational network and collaborative linkages), Hudson (1987) has suggested that there are five key factors which predispose agencies to collaborate. He highlights inter-organisational homogeneity – a similarity in values and beliefs; domain consensus – agreement on roles and responsibilities; network awareness; organisational exchange – a potential for all the parties to gain from working together; and an absence of alternative resources or the facility to access new resources. A major advantage can also be the existence of trust built up through previous joint activity.

The ingredients for successful partnership working have been specified further by Hudson and Hardy (2002). Building on their extensive empirical work and assisted by their application of the Partnership Assessment Tool (Hardy *et al.*, 2000) they have identified six generic partnership principles:

- *Acknowledgement of the need for partnership* – this includes the recognition of the interdependencies which make partnership working a sensible route.

- *Clarity and realism of purpose* – values and principles need to be agreed, and more specific aims and objectives to be achieved by the partnership need to be identified. A judgement needs to be made as to 'collaborative capacity', the extent of partnership working that is viable.

- *Commitment and ownership* – there needs to be consistent commitment from senior levels and ownership of the principles of partnership working at all levels of the organisations. The role of the 'champions' identified above may be important in this context.

- *Development and maintenance of trust* – this is particularly important for the maintenance of partnerships in the longer term. Equivalent status across all partners is important, together with the perception of fairness in the operation of the partnership.

- *Establishment of clear and robust partnership arrangements* – excessive bureaucracy needs to be avoided and straightforward procedures established. The focus should be on processes and outcomes rather than structures and inputs, and financial resources should be transparent.

- *Monitoring, review and organisational learning* – those working in partnership need to reflect on and evaluate their activities, to define factors of success and to monitor the extent to which they are achieved.

Although the Partnership Assessment Tool is not without its critics (Halliday *et al.*, 2004), and uses language that is not always readily accessible, it offers a useful summary indicator of areas of strength and weakness in partnership development. The tool also offers the opportunity for graphical presentation of the profile scores for each partnership site. The original formulation of the Partnership Assessment Tool envisaged two stages, the first a rapid appraisal and the second, where required, a more detailed and structured assessment. The scoring system for the first stage allows for four bands of development to be identified:

1. The partnership is working well enough in all or most aspects to make the need for a second stage assessment unlikely.
2. The partnership is working well overall but some aspects may need further exploration via a second stage assessment.
3. The partnership may be working well overall in some respects but these are outweighed by areas of concern sufficient to make a second stage assessment necessary.
4. The partnership is working badly enough in all respects for a second stage assessment to be essential.

Poxton (1999) has identified 'building blocks' considered essential to partnership working and has encapsulated them in what he has termed the Partnership Readiness Framework (Greig and Poxton, 2000):

- building and agreeing shared values and principles with a vision of how life should be for people who use services;
- agreeing specific policy shifts that the partnership arrangements are designed to achieve;
- being prepared to explore new service options and not be overly tied to existing services or providers;
- clarifying what aspects of service and activity are within the boundaries of the partnership arrangements – focus on real added value of joint working;
- being clear as to organisational roles in terms of responsibilities for and relationships between commissioning, purchasing and providing;
- identifying agreed resource pools, including pooled budgets – and putting aside unresolvable historical disagreements about financial responsibility;
- ensuring effective leadership, including political and other senior-level commitment to the partnership agenda;
- providing sufficient dedicated partnership developmental capacity rather than making it a small and marginalised part of everybody's role;
- developing and sustaining good personal relationships, creating opportunities and initiatives for key players to nurture those relationships in order to promote mutual trust.

Absence of these factors is likely to lead to difficulty in sustaining partnerships. In a more recent discussion, Poxton (2004) has suggested a framework of questions which can be used to define the particular model of partnership working that may be appropriate for a specific situation:

- What achievements are being sought?
- What is the local history of partnership working?

- What does the current organisational and political geography reveal?
- How does organisational reconfiguration affect partnership structures?
- How important is the current strength of local partnership(s)?
- How broad should the local partnership structure be?
- How should users, carers, the independent sector and local communities be involved in the partnership model? (pp. 20–21)

The evidence base for partnership working

A common-sense assumption might well be that partnership working is likely to be more effective in the delivery of desired objectives than two or more agencies operating on their own. Indeed, the policy drivers for partnership working are very much a manifestation of such assumptions. It is instructive to explore the evidence base for health and social care partnerships in more detail and to assess the extent to which it is robust. Evidence-based policy has been a policy driver for New Labour not dissimilar to the drive for partnership working. The nature of evidence, however, is very much an area of debate; indeed the politics of evidence ensure that to date there has rarely been consensus as to what counts as acceptable evidence.

Asthana *et al.* (2002) highlight the importance of identifying inputs, processes, outcomes and impacts as key analytical components, together with the context in which partnership working is taking place. The organisational level of the partnership (strategic, operational or front-line) and the stage of development of the partnership are also key. Glendinning (2002) suggests that the nature of partnerships requires a pluralistic approach to their evaluation. She draws on the framework developed by Thomas and Palfrey (1996) to suggest a number of core criteria against which to evaluate initiatives. These include effectiveness, efficiency, equity, acceptability, accessibility, appropriateness, accountability, ethics, responsiveness and choice, and implementation and roll-out. A range of considerations and challenges attach to each dimension. Villeneau *et al.* (2001) offer a framework for analysing joint working in mental health, identifying six key indicators and related criteria sourced from a national survey, while most recently Dickinson (2006) has suggested that a framework of what is termed 'critical realism' may assist with the challenge of relating outcome to process.

A number of early studies of health and social care partnerships sounded the first alert on the need for caution. A literature review by Cameron *et al.* (2000) concluded that there was a 'dearth of research evidence to support the notion that joint working between health and social care services is effective'. More recently, Dowling *et al.* (2004) have discussed in more detail the interpretations of success, either implicit or explicit, which are applied to partnership working. Their search of bibliographic databases for publications post 1997 identified 36 relevant articles. The majority of these have focused on the *process* of partnership working, for example the extent of common agreement as to the purpose of the partnership and the levels of trust and reciprocity. Few have looked in detail at the impact of partnership working in terms of whether it made a difference to those on its receiving end, in current parlance in terms of *outcomes*. This is a critical distinction and should be central to any discussion of the effectiveness of partnership working.

Discussion of outcomes inevitably raises issues of attribution. To what extent can it be assumed that the outcomes that are identified, whether at individual or service level, are a product of the activity under scrutiny? Is it partnership working that has produced the observed outcomes or could they have occurred as the result of other extraneous activity? In the context of partnership working, the traditional experimental method is often not feasible. It may be necessary, therefore, to rely on what would be traditionally termed 'most likely' explanations, or in more contemporary terminology 'theories of change', in order to relate particular activity to outcome (Sullivan *et al.*, 2002). It has been argued that the onus to specify such theories at the outset should assist in teasing out not only causal chains but interactions across the whole system. Health and social care systems are complex, open systems and what is being sought is a flexible approach that can embrace this complexity yet still say something of value (Barnes *et al.*, 2003).

In one of the few studies focusing on outcomes, Brown *et al.* (2002, 2003) compared two integrated health and social care teams for older people in Wiltshire with a traditional non-integrated team. An earlier study comparing different team models (Tucker and Brown, 1997) had concluded that 'at this point it is clear that the development of team working has more of an impact on staff than on users' (p. ii). This second study therefore addressed the impact for service users. The primary focus for comparison was the proportion of people remaining at home 18 months after referral. The rates for the integrated teams, however, were lower than for the traditional service. Moreover, quality of life scores were lower and depression levels higher for the integrated teams. There was some indication of higher levels of self-referral to the integrated teams and of more rapid assessment, but overall 'this research has not produced any findings which suggest that an integrated primary care-based health and social care team is more clinically effective than a traditional non-integrated method of service delivery' (p. 8).

This study also highlights, however, some of the challenges inherent in the evaluation of partnership working. Any evaluation takes place in a real world environment where practice rarely stands still: it will be evolving and modifying even as the comparisons are taking place. Likewise, models in practice often have less clarity and less distinction between them than those on paper: in the Wiltshire study, for example, it was suggested that the 'integrated' teams were more at the stage of co-location than integration, with staff still employed and managed by the separate agencies.

A second study that also suggests a need for caution in adopting assertions on the benefits of partnership working was reported by Peck *et al.* (2002). The study was an evaluation of the Somerset Partnerships Health and Social Care NHS Trust, established in 1999 as the first combined health and social care provider for mental health. The evaluation sought to identify the impact of joint commissioning and combined service provision on services users and carers, on professional staff, and on the agencies involved. A range of dimensions were explored at baseline and at one and two years post-implementation. Responses varied for the three groups. Service users, for example, reported improved mental health status and were more positive about the services they were receiving; they were critical, however, of the availability of support and access to buildings and had concerns over the attitudes of staff. Unpaid carers considered that some aspects of service delivery had improved, but felt that there were continuing problems around the identification and involvement of carers, both at the individual and agency level.

Responses from staff were varied. In the initial months there had been a reduction in job satisfaction, in morale and in role clarity. Two years after the formation of the Trust some of this was recovering, but there remained a number of areas of concern: organisational identity; role clarity and inter-disciplinary working; and leadership and management. Some staff, for example, were concerned at a lack of identity for the Trust, disgruntled with the management structure, and discomfited by the potential for changed relationships with colleagues. Likewise, although there were reports of some improvements in team environments and accounts of picking up skills from colleagues, boundaries between professionals remained. Workload and bureaucracy were perceived to have increased, there was concern as to the pressure on team managers, and anxiety among the smaller disciplines, for example occupational therapy, as to whether their views would be included.

Finally, from the perspective of the agencies there was concern as to whether the Joint Commissioning Board was fulfilling its role: there was a sense that core business was conducted elsewhere, and user and carer members questioned the extent to which they were being involved. There was considered to have been a lack of preparation for primary care involvement and uncertainty around the identity of the Trust. A fundamental issue was the 'culture' to be adopted by the partnership – whether it should be a new and different culture or an enhancement of the cultures already in place in the merging bodies (Peck *et al.*, 2001):

> Is the desired result one entirely new culture, albeit comprised of elements taken from all the current professional cultures – the melting pot approach to culture? Or is the desired result the enhancement of the current professional cultures by the addition of mutual understanding and respect – the orange juice with added vitamin 'c' approach to culture? (p. 325)

This is a key question and one that is often not fully resolved, potentially adding a further layer of uncertainty and confusion to the debates around partnership working.

El Ansari *et al.* (2001) provide a useful discussion of the complexities of establishing the evidence base. A number of factors are outlined. By its very nature, partnership working is going to involve a range of disciplines and a diversity of perspectives, and these multiple facets present a challenge to evaluation. As highlighted above, there will be difficulty in capturing the diverse factors that impact on the effectiveness of collaboration and a need to focus on the specifics of 'what works for whom under what circumstances'. Decisions have to be made as to whether any evaluation is conducted at a macro or micro level and the appropriate timescale for measuring any effects. Moreover, effects may be shorter or longer term. There is the challenge also of whether outcomes are explored at the individual or collective level: the complex nature of partnership activity and the environment within which it operates means that attribution of change to any particular intervention can be virtually impossible. The challenge of measuring a moving target has already been cited – 'today's barriers and obstacles, if challenged and crossed, become tomorrow's positive outcomes' (p. 220). They conclude, following their analysis, that 'collaboration is complex and enquiries into its effectiveness by different parties will be on the basis of different agendas with contrasting criteria and potentially conflicting perceptions' (p. 223).

In discussing partnership working, commentators often make reference to Northern Ireland, where health and personal social services have been delivered within an integrated structure of Health and Social Services Boards and Trusts since 1973. Surprisingly there has been no major evaluation of this service delivery and therefore much of the debate is anecdotal. Often this suggests that, although structural integration is in place, services separate out beneath the top levels. A study by Dornan (1999), however, which looked in detail at multidisciplinary team working with older people in Down Lisburn Trust, an integrated Health and Social Services Trust in the Eastern Health and Social Services Board area, found strong support for integrated teams. A range of indicators of collaborative working were investigated, including communication between disciplines, understanding of respective roles, the extent of co-operative working practices, access to files and information systems, shared objectives and philosophy, and the extent to which team members perceived themselves as relating to others as members of a common team. Findings were positive, with respondents judging professional autonomy and systems and the standing of their profession as good or better than previous arrangements. It was also considered that services to users and carers had improved, although it should be noted that this was a professional perception rather than a user response. Specific benefits cited were clarity over one entry point to all health and social care services; access to a wide range of community care services at a convenient location, usually within 15 minutes of home; and reduction in duplication and inflexible practice with, for example, a district nurse able to arrange home care or a care manager able to deliver continence products.

Glendinning *et al.* (2005) drew on two pieces of research to explore the argument further. The first focused on the development of partnerships between primary care groups and trusts and local authorities, while the second explored the early use of the flexibilities introduced under the Health Act 1999. The successive surveys in the first study revealed some changes in service delivery, particularly the development of intermediate care and rehabilitation initiatives. The authors were not able, however, to demonstrate that the partnerships necessarily led to better services or to improved outcomes for either providers or service users. Similarly, while the study of the first phase of Health Act flexibilities (Glendinning *et al.*, 2002) revealed changes in the relationships between partners, more substantive evidence in terms of impact was not available:

> . . . the available research evidence is still limited and, moreover, is unable to demonstrate that these outputs could not be achieved in other ways (which might also involve lower net costs); or that they lead to improved outcomes or benefits for service users, other stakeholders or the wider society. (p. 374)

A recent study was designed to look specifically at whether health and social care partnerships are delivering the outcomes valued by service users (Petch *et al.*, 2007). These outcomes built upon those identified through a research programme at the Social Policy Research Unit (Qureshi, 2001). Although this was less concerned with questions as to whether partnerships alone could deliver these outcomes, it does offer some tentative conclusions that associate particular outcomes with specific features of partnership working. Analysis of the findings from this project demonstrated firstly that the 15 health and social care partnerships were effective in delivering good outcomes as defined by service users.

More importantly for the current context, the accounts from service users allowed the identification of key features of services delivered in partnership that had a particularly positive impact. These included continuity of staff and sufficient staff, good resources, and the availability of preventative and long-term services, enabling fluid support matched to the needs of the user. Furthermore, the user accounts allowed the identification of key features of partnership that shaped service delivery in ways that supported the outcomes that service users valued. These are summarised in Table 1.1 below.

This initial chapter has highlighted the complex and multi-faceted nature of partnership working. It has exposed the aspirations lurking behind the concept and has detailed a range of analytical frameworks that have been put forward. Finally, it has suggested that, although there may be some

Table 1.1 Features of partnerships and related outcomes

Key features of partnership	Related features of services	Outcomes delivered
Co-location of staff	Providing a single point of contact, improving access and communication	• Process outcomes, especially responsiveness • Quality of life outcome: feeling safe
Multidisciplinary team	Providing holistic care	• Change outcomes • Quality of life outcomes • Process outcomes
Specialist partnership	Providing specialist, non-discriminatory treatment	• Process outcomes, especially being treated with respect
Extended partnership	Providing access to other agencies, and partnership with service users	• Quality of life outcomes, including activity and contact with other people • Process outcome: having choices

embryonic whispers of a more promising nature, the evidence base in support of partnership working delivering more effective outcomes is flimsy.

CHAPTER 2

The UK Context
for Partnership Working

I think people do need to work together, so that it's not a case
of the right hand not knowing what the left hand's doing.

This chapter traces the development of the partnership working agenda prior to devolution and then outlines how it has evolved in the rest of the UK post devolution. Despite the somewhat uncertain evidence base outlined in Chapter One, a drive for partnership working has been a major feature of the modernisation agenda introduced by the Labour government in 1997. This is often portrayed as a response to the fragmentation and disjunction seen to have resulted from the earlier emphasis on a market-driven system (see, for example, Glendinning *et al.*, 2002). The new government wished to move from the competitive contract culture to a more inclusive partnership approach, in both the public and private sectors.

Initiatives in partnership working have waxed and waned over what Lewis (2001) has characterised as 'half a century of hidden policy conflict'. She has traced the elements of three key divisions – financial, administrative and professional – in what she has termed 'a constant battle between the two services over the kind of needs they would meet'. It is of course the financial implications that impact most starkly on the individual: support defined as 'health care' is provided free at the point of delivery to the individual, whereas for 'social care' support there will generally be some form of means-tested charge. Broader financial implications merge with the administrative in the form of 'cost shunting' between health and social care and in the spectre of delayed transfers of care from hospital beds. Professional divisions have long been caricatured in the debates as to what constitutes the 'health bath' and the 'social care bath'.

With the creation of the National Health Service under the 1946 Act, separate identities were granted to GPs as independent contractors, to hospital services, and to local authority public health departments, including environmental health and community nurses. The proposal for a unified local government health service had been unacceptable to the medical profession. Twenty years later the 1964 Kilbrandon Committee in Scotland and the 1965 Seebohm Committee in England heralded the first comprehensive approach to local authority social services.

The National Health Service Act 1973 finalised the separation of health and social care by removing public health (including community nursing) to a unified health structure. At the same time, however, a mechanism for joint health and social care planning was created through member-based joint consultative committees, with parallel forums for professionals established from 1976. The same year saw the creation of joint finance possibilities, with NHS monies top-sliced to support local authority projects.

These initiatives of the seventies advanced only slowly through the eighties. Joint planning proved disappointing: in Scotland it was characterised in the title of a report, *Stop ... Start ... Stutter* (Kohls, 1989). Joint financing was modest, and together with joint planning was being by-passed by the availability of residential care monies from the Department of Health and Social Security (DHSS), which were unlimited by any requirement for a needs assessment. Joint consultative committees and joint care planning teams around hospital closure continued through the eighties, but the groundwork for more recent developments started to be laid with the 1986 Audit Commission report *Making a Reality of Community Care*, and the subsequent Griffiths Report in 1988, *Community Care: An Agenda for Action* (DHSS, 1988). This signalled an end, in respect of partnership working, to the 'discredited refuge of imploring collaboration and exhorting action'.

The NHS and Community Care Act 1990, which followed the Griffiths Report and the White Paper *Caring for People,* placed a requirement on local health authorities and local authorities to jointly develop community care plans which would include the development of joint strategies and service objectives, the specification of needs assessments and agreed hospital discharge plans, and the development of joint commissioning. Early pursuit of these new goals can be seen in the promotion of joint commissioning (Department of Health, 1995), particularly for mental health and learning disability (Department of Health, 1997a).

A study conducted during this period by Hiscock and Pearson (1999) sought to understand the perspectives of health and social care professionals on the partnership working initiatives. In-depth interviews were conducted with 98 professionals in four case study sites in the north-west of England. Two key features among front-line professionals were identified at this time. The first was the continuing and deteriorating gap between the two services; the second was the inward focus on the instability and change within their own organisations, pre-empting the development of external links – 'a low priority for professionals feeling stretched to the limits by other aspects of the health and social care reforms' (p. 156). These included changing workloads, new demands and expectations imposed by the market reforms, and fears about job security. Despite the policy directives, the real-world experience was somewhat different. There was not sufficient recognition, the authors argue, of the size of the gap, and the professionals – social workers, GPs, community nurses, home care workers – worked in parallel rather than jointly. There were concerns about unnegotiated care and cost shifting and there was a wariness of the practices of other professionals. Hiscock and Pearson provide a stark empirical account which offers a sobering rejoinder to the exhortations for collaboration and partnership working.

The policy milestones of the New Labour modernisation agenda post 1997 can be sketched in a little more detail. In England, the White Paper *The New NHS: Modern, Dependable* heralded an NHS led by primary care (Department of Health, 1997b). It recommended the abolition of GP fund-holding and the internal market in health, and sought to expand the role of GPs as service commissioners. Primary Care Groups became Primary Care Trusts (PCTs). At the same time the government pledged to bring down what was characterised as the 'Berlin Wall' between health and social care (Glasby, 2003). The White Paper introduced a new duty of partnership 'so that local health services pull together rather than pull apart'.

In 1998, *Modernising Social Services* (Department of Health, 1998a) switched from the notion of major reorganisation towards 'fostering a new spirit of flexible partnership working which moves away from sterile con-flicts over boundaries to an approach where this wasted time and effort is directed positively towards working across them'. Incentive strategies, for example Joint Investment Plans, were put in place to improve joint working between health and social care and to avoid unnecessary hospital admis-sions. In the same year, for the first time the Department of Health presented combined national priorities across health and social care (Department of Health, 1998b). The House of Commons Health Committee (1998) under-took an inquiry into the relationship between health and social services. This led to 30 wide-ranging recommendations designed to promote closer working, and a full response from the government (Department of Health, 1999b). The view that 'the government does not believe it is necessary to formally integrate health and social services' was reiterated.

In September 1998 the Department of Health issued for discussion a document titled *Partnership in Action (New Opportunities for Joint Working between Health and Social Services)* (Department of Health, 1998c). This recognised the 'no man's land between health and social services', but declared firmly that new authorities combining health and social care would not be established: 'major structural change is not the answer'. Moreover, piecemeal attention to individual elements such as joint planning needed to be replaced by a whole system approach embracing strategic planning, service commissioning and service provision. *Partnership in Action* sought:

- a clarification of the purpose of the partnership;
- recognition and resolution of areas of conflict;
- agreement on a shared approach to partnership;
- development of strong leadership;

- continuous adaptation to reflect the lessons learned from the experience;
- incentives to reward effective working across organisational (and geographical) boundaries.

The discussion document indicated the intention of introducing legislative powers designed to remove barriers to joint working and to accelerate the demolition of the 'Berlin Wall'. These powers materialised in Section 31 of the Health Act 1999. This removed the existing legal barriers to allow the promotion of pooled budgets, of lead commissioning and of integrated provision. These initiatives have become known as the 'Health Act flexibilities'. A range of initiatives targeting similar objectives were introduced during the same period. These include Health Action Zones (Barnes *et al.*, 2005), the requirement to work in partnership to improve the health and well-being of the local population under Health Improvement Plans (Department of Health, 1997b), and the representation of local authorities on primary care groups and PCTs. At the same time additional resources were made available, including the creation of a £647 million Partnership Grant under the Social Services Modernisation Fund to 'foster partnerships between health and social services in promoting independence'.

The three flexibilities introduced by the Health Act 1999 were designed to facilitate partnership working through removing barriers which could inhibit effective service delivery. *Pooled budgets* involve the allocation of funds to a mutual pot which can then be accessed through the budget manager without the necessity for lengthy determination as to whether the proposed use of the funds should be defined as health or social care. Under *lead commissioning*, one authority delegates responsibility to the other which can then purchase the necessary support irrespective of whether it is health or social care. *Integrated provision* allows services to be integrated within a single organisation, a 'one-stop shop', in order to deliver more comprehensive and streamlined support. Alternatively, specific services may be transferred to another partner, for example community nursing for older people might be placed within the local authority.

The operation of the Health Act flexibilities has been explored in two major evaluations. The first (Glendinning *et al.*, 2004, 2005) examined initial notifications of use of the flexibilities which came into force in April 2000. Early indications were not favourable in terms of numbers, with only 20 authorities taking up the discretionary opportunity at the initial implementation date. Scrutiny initially of the first 32 notifications and then of all those received in the first two years showed that pooled budgets were the most popular flexibility. They were most often used in the early months for services for people with learning disabilities, older people – particularly for intermediate care and for 'rapid response' services – and people with mental health problems, but over time their use was extended to other groups and new partners. Areas which proved problematic included the sharing of information, in part due to IT incompatibilities; cultural differences between partners; and resource constraints. The flexibility allowing integrated provision encountered most difficulties in implementation. The authors concluded that three factors were key to success: strong, visible leadership and commitment; time; and attention to local conditions and histories.

Not everything, however, was solved by the introduction of the Health Act flexibilities. For example, Glendinning *et al.* (2004) found that, despite operating pooled budgets, agencies were required to report separately on activity and expenditure. This requirement for disaggregation of what had been operated as a joint activity seemed to undermine the core principles behind the introduction of the flexibilities.

The second evaluation of the Health Act flexibilities was conducted by Phelps *et al.* under the Modernising Adult Social Care research initiative. This sought to determine the extent to which the use of the flexibilities promoted effective partnership working and positive outcomes for frail older people. It revealed substantial discrepancies between Department of Health notification data on Health Act flexibilities and data returned to the Commission for Social Care Inspection (CSCI). The Department of Health data confirmed the predominance of one type of flexibility: pooled budgets were involved in over three quarters of the notifications, either on their own (45 per cent) or in combination (a further 34 per cent). Data from three case study sites suggested that the factors that facilitated uptake were government policy drivers, senior management commitment, and the adoption of a whole systems approach. The employment of external expertise or dedicated staff to project manage the process was also an advantage. Barriers to the process included resistance from senior management and the time-consuming and bureaucratic nature of the notification procedures. One site not using Health Act flexibilities had been reluctant to relinquish financial control into pooled budgets.

Since the beginning of the new century there has been an acceleration of the policy directives in England promoting partnership. *The NHS Plan: A Plan for Investment, a Plan for Reform* (Department of Health, 2000) envisaged a central role for primary care and proposed a new level of PCT, a Care Trust which 'will be able to commission and deliver primary and community health care as well as social care for older people and other client groups. Social services would be delivered under delegated authority from local councils.' Permissive legislation enabling the creation of Care Trusts was brought forward in the 2001 Health and Social Care Act. This same Act also placed a 'duty of partnership' on each agency and allowed for the use of Health Act flexibilities to be enforced in an area if health and social care were not deemed to be adequately working together, further strengthening the partnership imperative. The proposal in *The NHS Plan* to enforce the creation of a Care Trust where health and social care organisations fail to establish effective partnerships did not make it to legislation. Glasby (2003) suggests that the proposals at this time reflect an uneasy mix of incentive and compulsion:

> In many ways, this seems to be the worst of all worlds – neither the enforced amalgamation feared by local authorities, nor the retention of separate professional identities; neither outright central compulsion, nor an overwhelming vote of confidence in local discretion. (p. 974)

Contributors to Glasby and Peck (2004) have looked in detail at the development of Care Trusts. Relatively few areas have pursued the Care Trust model; at the time of writing the numbers remain in single figures. This is a significant shift from the prospect of the 'final countdown' to radical restructuring explored by the commentary of Hudson and Henwood (2002). This reflected the declaration by the then Health Minister that he expected all adult social care services to be delivered by Care Trusts within five years; inclusion of housing was also proposed.

National Service Frameworks

As part of the government's agenda to drive up standards and reduce unacceptable variations in health and social services, a series of National Service Frameworks have been developed.

Mental health

The *National Service Framework for Mental Health* published in 1999 (Department of Health, 1999a) was one of the first two frameworks, delivered alongside coronary heart disease. It addresses the mental health needs of those aged up to 65. It provides the detail for the policies of the White Paper, *Modernising Mental Health Services* (Department of Health, 1998d) and is driven by ten guiding values and principles:

- Involve service users and their carers in planning and delivery of care.
- Deliver high quality treatment and care which is known to be effective and acceptable.
- Be well suited to those who use them and non-discriminatory.
- Be accessible so that help can be obtained when and where it is needed.
- Promote their safety and that of their carers, staff and the wider public.
- Offer choices which promote independence.
- Be well co-ordinated between all staff and agencies.
- Deliver continuity of care for as long as this is needed.
- Empower and support their staff.

- Be properly accountable to the public, service users and carers.

Detailed scrutiny of the evidence base underpins the framework, with each evidence source classified according to the nature of the study methodology on a Type 1 to Type 5 basis. Seven standards were set:

One   *Mental health promotion*
Standard: Health and social services should a) promote mental health for all, working with individuals and communities and b) combat discrimination against individuals and groups with mental health problems, and promote their social inclusion.

Two   *Primary care and access to services*
Standard: Any service user who contacts their primary health care team with a common mental health problem should a) have their mental health needs identified and assessed, and b) be offered effective treatments, including referral to specialist services for further assessment, treatment and care if they require it.

Three   *Primary care and access to services*
Standard: Any individual with a common mental health problem should a) be able to make contact round the clock with the local services necessary to meet their needs and receive adequate care, and b) be able to use NHS Direct, as it develops, for first-level advice and referral on to specialist helplines or to local services.

Four   *Effective services for people with severe mental illness*
Standard: All mental health service users on CPA (the Care Programme Approach) should a) receive care which optimises engagement, anticipates or prevents a crisis, and reduces risk, and b) have a copy of a written care plan which includes the action to be taken in a crisis by the service user, their carer, and their care co-ordinator; advises their GP how they should respond if the service user needs additional help; is regularly reviewed by their care co-ordinator; [and allows access to] services 24 hours a day, 365 days a year.

Five   *Effective services for people with severe mental illness*
Standard: Each service user who is assessed as requiring a period of care away from their home should have a) timely access to an appropriate hospital bed or alternative bed or place, which is in the least restrictive environment consistent with the need to protect them and the public [and is] as close to home as possible, and b) a copy of a written after-care plan agreed on discharge which sets out the care and rehabilitation to be provided, identifies the care co-ordinator, and specifies the action to be taken in a crisis.

Six   *Caring about carers*
Standard: All individuals who provide regular and substantial care for a person on CPA should a) have an assessment of their caring, physical and mental health needs, repeated on at least an annual basis, and b) have their own written care plan which is given to them and implemented in discussion with them.

Seven   *Preventing suicide*
Standard: Local health and social care communities could prevent suicides by: promoting mental health for all, working with individuals and communities (Standard one); delivering high quality primary mental health care (Standard two); ensuring that anyone with a mental health problem can contact local services via the primary care team, a helpline or an A&E department (Standard three); ensuring that individuals with severe and enduring mental illness have a care plan which meets their specific needs, including access to services round the clock (Standard four); providing safe hospital accommodation for individuals who need it (Standard five); enabling individuals caring for someone with severe mental illness to receive the support which they need to continue to care (Standard six); and they should in addition support local prison staff in preventing suicides among prisoners; ensure that staff are competent to assess the risk of suicide among individual at greatest risk; and develop local systems for suicide audit to learn lessons and take any necessary action.

The detail of these standards confirms that a multi-agency and multi-professional response to the needs of those with mental ill health is essential. The framework also stresses the importance of a common vision and strategy at the local level:

> Local health and social care communities will need to assess the current interfaces between all health organisations and local government departments, and determine how best to fulfil the Duty of Partnership, deploying the new flexibilities to achieve the national standards, and to demonstrate progress against local milestones. (p. 84)

Mental health was for the first time made a shared national priority for health and social services in the National Priorities Guidance for 1999/00–2001/02. It was recognised that 'delivering the National Service Framework will require new patterns of local partnership, with mental health a cross cutting priority for all NHS and social care organisations and their partners' (p. 6), and an additional £700 million was allocated under *Modernising Mental Health Services* to 'help local health and social care communities reshape mental health services' (p. 7). The necessity of a whole system approach to mental health was emphasised, and health and social care services were encouraged to consider the range of alternatives for commissioning services. One option was a Joint Commissioning Board, including the local authority, health authority and primary care group. An alternative option was a lead commissioner, either local authority, primary care group or trust, or health authority.

Older people

The *National Service Framework for Older People* was published in 2001 (Department of Health, 2001a), 'the first ever comprehensive strategy to ensure fair, high quality, integrated health and social care services for older people'. It was acknowledged that 'organisational structures have acted to impede the provision of care co-ordinated around the needs of the older person' (p. 8), and use of the Health Act flexibilities was encouraged 'to ensure an integrated approach to service provision, such that they are person-centred, regardless of professional or organisational boundaries' (p. 9). Specific developments were the introduction of a single needs assessment process across health and social care; improved access to community equipment; and development of integrated continence services. Standards were set for the support of older people across health and social services, irrespective of whether people are in their own homes, in hospital, or in a care home. Principles underpinning the framework include rooting out age discrimination; providing person-centred care; promoting older people's health and independence; and fitting services around people's needs. The eight standards are as follows.

One   *Rooting out age discrimination*
Standard   NHS services will be provided, regardless of age, on the basis of clinical need alone. Social care services will not use age in their eligibility criteria or policies, to restrict access to available services.

Two   *Person-centred care*
Standard   NHS and social care services treat older people as individuals and enable them to make choices about their own care. This is achieved through the single assessment process, integrated commissioning arrangements and integrated provision of services, including community equipment and continence services.

Three   *Intermediate Care*
Standard   Older people will have access to a new range of intermediate care services at home or in designated care settings, to promote their independence by providing enhanced services from the NHS and councils to prevent unnecessary hospital admission, and effective rehabilitation services to enable early discharge from hospital

and to prevent premature or unnecessary admission to long-term residential care.

Four   *General hospital care*
Standard   Older people's care in hospital is delivered through appropriate specialist care and by hospital staff who have the right set of skills to meet their needs.

Five   *Stroke*
Standard   The NHS will take action to prevent strokes, working in partnership with other agencies where appropriate. People who are thought to have had a stroke have access to diagnostic services, are treated appropriately by a specialist stroke service, and subsequently, with their carers, participate in a multidisciplinary programme of secondary prevention and rehabilitation.

Six   *Falls*
Standard   The NHS, working in partnership with councils, takes action to prevent falls and reduce resultant fractures or other injuries in their populations of older people. Older people who have fallen receive effective treatment and, with their carers, receive advice on prevention through a specialised falls service.

Seven   *Mental health in older people*
Standard   Older people who have mental health problems have access to integrated mental health services, provided by the NHS and councils to ensure effective diagnosis, treatment and support, for them and for their carers.

Eight   *The promotion of health and active life in older age*
Standard   The health and well-being of older people is promoted through a co-ordinated programme of action led by the NHS with support from councils.

For each standard a number of potential key interventions are highlighted, together with milestones, dates by which certain targets and activities are to be completed. The eight standards of the *National Service Framework for Older People* are again characterised by detailed specification of the evidence base from which they have been constructed. The specific targets can be equated with service-based outcomes. Perhaps less explicit are the specific outcomes for individuals expected from each standard, although at least some of these are implicit in the prescribed action. In addition, the standards of the National Service Framework are being linked to both the NHS and Personal Social Services Performance Assessment Frameworks.

Progress on each of the standards will not be explored in detail. Anticipating the discussion in later chapters, however, it is interesting to note the extent to which target dates slip. For example, the initial milestone for the introduction of the Single Assessment Process under Standard Two was April 2002, while by April 2004 single integrated community equipment services and continence services were to be in place. The Single Assessment Process has now been reframed as the Common Assessment Framework, and implementation remains patchy.

The provision of intermediate care (Standard Three) is of particular interest in the context of health and social care. A National Beds Inquiry in 2000 had investigated the long-standing issue of the extent to which older people were remaining in acute hospital beds when their primary need was for social care. As acute bed numbers were reduced, widespread practice was to transfer frail older people into residential and nursing home settings. A major role for rehabilitation services was identified (Audit Commission, 2000) and the provision of what has been termed 'intermediate care' became a priority of *The NHS Plan* (Department of Health, 2000). Guidance was issued in January 2001, a financial allocation made (£900 million annually by 2003/04 for intermediate care and related services to promote independence) and initial targets were set. By March 2004 there were to be at least 5000 additional intermediate care beds and 1700 non-residential intermediate care places on the 1999/2000 baseline; at least 150,000 additional people receiving intermediate care services promoting rehabilitation and supported discharge; and at least 70,000 additional people receiving intermediate care which prevents unnecessary hospital admission. The Community Care (Delayed Discharge etc.) Act 2003 removed local authorities' ability to charge for community equipment and intermediate care services, removing any barrier to joint provision with health.

At the mid-point of the ten-year National Service Framework a progress report, *Living Well in Later Life,* was produced by the Healthcare Commission, the Audit Commission and the CSCI (Commission for Healthcare Audit and Inspection, 2006). The first joint report from the three inspection bodies, it was based on evidence from inspection of the whole system of services in ten communities. The eight standards of the framework were grouped into five cross-cutting themes, with an emphasis on the three conditions in the framework, stroke, falls and mental health. While some progress was identified, further action in three key areas was considered essential to improve the service experiences of older people. The three areas were tackling discrimination through ageist attitudes; ensuring all the standards in the National Service Framework are met, and strengthening partnership working. In respect of the latter, it was felt that there was a lack of shared direction across the agencies, leading to fragmentation and an inconsistent and unco-ordinated range of services:

> Sustainable change cannot take place unless all partner organisations have a shared view of the direction in which they want to move, and how they plan to get there. (p. 86)

Learning disability

The key policy document addressing the support of people with learning disabilities is not a National Service Framework but a White Paper, *Valuing People: A New Strategy for Learning Disability for the 21st Century* (Department of Health, 2001b). This was issued in March 2001 and sought to address the many areas of the lives of people with learning disabilities where experiences were poor. A new vision was detailed, built around four core principles: rights as citizens; opportunities for independence; choice in daily life; and social inclusion in local communities. Monies were made available in the form of a new Learning Disability Development Fund of £50 million a year from April 2002; the fund was to be accessed as pooled funds under the Health Act flexibilities. In the context of the current discussion, the key element was the recognition that 'effective partnership working by all agencies is the key to achieving social inclusion for people with learning disabilities'. Specifically, Learning Disability Partnership Boards were to be established within the framework of Local Strategic Partnerships by October 2001. Partnership Boards were to take responsibility for implementing the White Paper, and for agreeing plans for the use of the Health Act flexibilities, and were charged with developing local action plans to supplement learning disability Joint Investment Plans.

Objective 1:   *Maximising Opportunities for Disabled Children*
To ensure that disabled children gain maximum life chance benefits from educational opportunities, health care and social care, while living with their families or in other appropriate settings in the community where their assessed needs are adequately met and reviewed.

Objective 2:   *Transition into adult life*
As young people with learning disabilities move into adulthood, to ensure continuity of care and support for the young person and their family and to provide equality of opportunity in order to enable as many disabled young people as possible to participate in education, training or employment.

Objective 3:   *Enabling people to have more control over their own lives*
To enable people with learning disabilities to have as much choice and control as possible over their lives through advocacy and a person-centred approach to planning the services they need.

Objective 4:   *Supporting carers*
To increase the help and support carers receive from all local agencies in order to fulfil their family and caring roles effectively.

Objective 5:   *Good health*
To enable people with learning disabilities to access a health service designed around their individual needs, with fast and convenient care delivered to a consistently high standard, and with additional support where necessary.

Objective 6:   *Housing*
To enable people with learning disabilities and their families to have greater choice and control over where, and how they live.

Objective 7:   *Fulfilling lives*
To enable people with learning disabilities to lead full and purposeful lives in their communities and to develop a range of friendships, activities and relationships.

Objective 8:   *Moving into employment*
To enable more people with learning disabilities to participate in all forms of employment, wherever possible in paid work and to make a valued contribution to the world of work.

Objective 9:   *Quality*
To ensure that all agencies commission and provide high quality, evidence based and continuously improving services which promote both good outcomes and best value.

Objective 10: *Workforce training and planning*
To ensure that social and health care staff working with people with learning disabilities are appropriately skilled, trained and qualified, and to promote a better understanding of the needs of people with learning disabilities amongst the wider workforce.

Objective 11: *Partnership working*
To promote holistic services for people with learning disabilities through effective partnership working between all relevant local agencies in the commissioning and delivery of services.

Although this last objective explicitly addresses partnership working, it is, as for mental health and for older people above, an essential prerequisite for successful achievement of the majority of the objectives. As the White Paper makes clear, 'people with learning disabilities and their families need to have confidence that all organisations are working together to achieve integrated service planning and commissioning, and that they can gain access to their choice of services through one clear access route' (p. 107). In addition to the responsibilities identified above, the Learning Disability Partnership Boards were charged with overseeing the planning and commissioning of integrated services offering a choice of support options, and with ensuring a smooth transition to adult life for young people with learning disabilities. Boards were also required to ensure that people with learning disabilities and carers are able to make a real contribution to the Board; that the cultural diversity of the community is reflected in the Board; and that local independent providers and the voluntary sector are fully engaged. Boards were likely to be led by the local council; where there were indications that effective partnerships had not been established, use of the new powers of the Health and Social Care Act 2001 to direct the use of partnership arrangements and to require the development of a Care Trust would be considered.

Keys to Partnership (Department of Health, 2002), guidance focusing on the partnership working necessary to achieve the White Paper objectives, was produced by the Department of Health. A number of key messages are spelt out. These include the need for partnership working to serve a purpose rather than exist for its own sake, the purpose in this case being a set of outcomes designed to improve life for people with learning disabilities. A willingness to share power and to work to an agreed agenda are seen as essential, together with a planned and phased approach which will take time. The breadth of the partnership required is emphasised, a partnership that embraces employment, leisure, housing and the independent sector, in addition to people with learning disabilities and their families. Elements of a partnership development framework are detailed, together with guidelines on how to audit a partnership, and suggestions on how to develop an effective Partnership Board. The notion of a managed care network, a parallel development to the managed clinical network, is advanced.

As indicated above, Learning Disability Partnership Boards were established within the framework of Local Strategic Partnerships and within the context of an overall national policy for partnership working which includes Health Improvement and Modernisation Partnerships, Health Action Zones, Education Action Zones, Better Government for Older People, Supporting People, and the work of the Social Inclusion Unit. Indeed under the Local Government Act 2000 (Local Government (Scotland) Act 2003), partnership working is considered key to all local authority functions, not just social care. Under the rubric of community planning, all the different sectors are expected to work together to empower communities.

Local Strategic Partnerships were required under the Local Government Act 2000 and have been operational since Spring 2002. They are intended to bring together different parts of the public sector and private, business, voluntary and community sectors in order to implement a community strategy for the area. Local plans, partnerships and initiatives are to be brought together to deliver a local neighbourhood renewal strategy. In turn the broader strategic agenda was reflected in the Strategic Partnerships Taskforce of the then Office of the Deputy Prime Minister and the formation of Strategic Service Partnerships (SSPs) – 'collaborative partnerships on ways of working between two or more partners of which at least one is a public sector body where the customer/user/community provide the main focus for the integrated delivery of strategic services'. Twenty-four Pathfinder projects, eight from each of five themes, were developed. One of the five themes was Education, Social Service and Health (ESH). Amongst its eight projects were the following:

- Barnsley Council and Barnsley PCT – integrated social care services;
- Manchester Council (Education, Social Services) and three PCTs (North, South and Central) – integrated children's services;
- Stockton and North Tees – integrated social services;
- Tameside Council and Glossop PCT (plus Tameside and Glossop Acute Services NHS Trust, Pennine Care Mental Health Trust and Tameside Health Partnership and Modernisation Board) – integrated elderly person services.

An evaluation was conducted of the Pathfinder projects (presentation by the Strategic Partnering Taskforce of the Office of the Deputy Prime Minister to the Integrated Care Network on 22 Jan 2004). Across all five themes, dimensions identified as key included leadership; communication and consultation; a formal assessment and development process; skills development; a formal review process; new resources; governance and scrutiny; market intelligence and experience; project management; working across central government; incremental strategic partnering; joint service delivery; minimising bidding and process costs; removing barriers and restrictions; and harnessing the skills of the voluntary, community and social enterprise sectors. Dimensions specific to the Education, Social Service and Health theme were incremental development; joint working structures (ranging from informal to Section 31); pooled budgets; development of children's partnerships and Children's Trusts; conditions of service and pensions; and investment funding. Interestingly there was not found to be the same degree of contention within this theme as within others.

A report from the King's Fund (Banks, 2002) titled *Partnerships under Pressure* offered a commentary on the progress in partnership working between the NHS and local government at that date. It drew on the discussions of an expert group and was encouraged by progress. Nine areas of concern, however, were identified and recommendations were advanced to address these issues. Areas of positive progress included the rationale for partnerships no longer being questioned; appreciation of the need for a whole systems approach; increased working together to produce joint strategies and plans; the development of new forms of integrated teams; and the emergence of different models of integrated care for different service users. One challenge to the development of partnership working was the increasing emphasis on 'hospitals in crisis' and the need to reduce emergency admissions and delayed discharges, exemplified in the introduction of the reimbursement system between local authorities and health systems. Other challenges were the presence of a number of perverse incentives reflected in audit and performance management systems; continuing reorganisation; barriers to cultural change at the front line; and resource pressures. The latter have been most dramatically demonstrated in recent developments in areas such as Wiltshire and Brent where key elements of partnership working have been dismantled as a result of financial crises in health. The discussion high-lights the damage inflicted on innovative partnerships 'who see their shared agenda high-jacked [sic] to serve the interest of the acute sector who are often the least concerned with partnerships' (p. 3).

The nine recommendations put forward at this time by the King's Fund for supporting partnerships can be summarised as follows:

- Local partnerships need to be given time to develop, free from further initiatives or structural change.
- Review of performance assessment indicators needs to check their relevance to partnership outcomes and remove duplication.
- Incentives rather than penalties should drive partnership working.
- The under-resourcing of social services needs to be addressed as this inhibits the partnership agenda.
- Further organisational changes should be resisted to allow for the establishment of PCTs and the modernisation of services.
- The change process itself needs to be resourced, in particular leadership development for middle managers.
- Central support should be provided for the development of common terms and conditions, information management, and technology systems.
- Users should be supported to participate fully in the development of partnerships.
- The impact of partnerships should be assessed in terms of the outcomes for service users and their carers.

Rummery (2003) and Rummery and Coleman (2003) report on a study designed to explore the development of partnership working between primary care groups or trusts and social services departments in England. This focused on provision for older people and explored the six principles of the Partnership Assessment Tool outlined in Chapter One (Hardy *et al.*, 2000). They concluded that progress towards partnership working between local authorities and the new primary care organisations had been variable over their first two years. A statutory requirement for local authority representation on the health bodies had assisted understanding; progress in terms of joint commissioning, however, was less evident. Moreover there was not, as yet, evidence of benefit for service users. The study also highlighted the need to acknowledge and work through differences between health and social care professionals and to obtain commitment from the wider organisation if robust partnerships are to be developed. The enthusiasm for partnership working, moreover, needs to be from both sides, with both partners believing they stand to benefit.

This overview of the context for partnership working in England suggests that, although the drive for partnership working has become a familiar feature of much recent policy, the delivery remains uncertain. Moreover, despite increasingly detailed evidence of the outcomes desired by service users, the extent to which partnership policies are framed in terms of achieving these outcomes is still tentative.

CHAPTER 3

The Development of the Joint Future Group and its Agenda in Scotland

I was shunted from pillar to post. I felt like a carrier pigeon to be honest.

This chapter will switch the focus back to Scotland. It will outline the development of partnership working in Scotland in the period prior to the creation of the Joint Future Group, and will explore the reasons for establishing the Joint Future Group, the recommendations from the group's report and the initial stages of implementation. A definitive account of the related legislation and circulars will be provided.

The Scottish context

The arrival of devolved government with the creation of the Scottish Parliament in 1999 has triggered a number of commentaries on the impact on health and social care policy (Greer, 2001; Carter and Woods, 2003; Stewart, 2004; Mooney and Scott, 2005). It is important to remember, however, that for many years there had been an element of independence within the Scottish system, with a number of key portfolios held at the Scottish Executive (and former Scottish Office).

The new Labour government of 1997, with its commitment to a modernisation agenda, is an appropriate baseline. In that year a White Paper, *Designed to Care: Renewing the National Health Service in Scotland* (Scottish Office, 1997a), was published. In tune with modernisation principles, this declared a key role for partnership working:

> the Government have concluded that a partnership approach based on co-operation, not competition, is the way ahead for Scotland's Health Service. A market-style NHS has failed patients; it set doctor against doctor, and developed two-tierism allied to bureaucracy, although to a lesser extent in Scotland than elsewhere. (para. 8)

Four partnerships were envisaged to deliver a patient-focused service:

- a partnership between the Government and the people of Scotland, reflected in the Government's pledge to continue with annual real increases in NHS funding;

- a partnership between patients and the professionals who care for them, by giving both a bigger say in the design and management of the NHS in Scotland;

- a partnership between different parts of the NHS in Scotland to promote the integration of care and provide patients with a seamless service;
- a partnership between the NHS in Scotland and other organisations whose work can help improve health and the quality of services to patients.

The White Paper outlined the development of PCTs, co-ordinating the delivery of primary health care across community hospitals, mental health services and networks of GPs in Local Health Care Co-operatives (LHCCs). The latter were to replace GP fundholding (relatively under-developed in Scotland), and to be based on 'natural communities'. Although there was no compulsion for LHCCs to have social care on board, it is interesting to note that a survey showed that by July 2001, 44 per cent had local authority links. It was recognised that PCTs would need to work closely with social work and with housing, particularly around the production of Health Improvement Plans (HIPs). The long legacy was acknowledged:

> There has been much debate about where the boundary between NHS care and care led by social work should rest. Whatever the structure, some boundary will inevitably exist. The important principle must be that the patient's care comes first. The patient should not perceive the boundary as interfering with the care he or she receives. To achieve this, the NHS in Scotland and local authorities need to develop close working relationships.

The Scottish Office Department of Health had already announced in circular MEL(1997)57 funding of £500k for a Local Care Partnerships Scheme. Six pilot initiatives were to be funded, 'to assist Health Boards and other relevant agencies to remove administrative or other barriers to effective and efficient local integration of health, housing and social care services in the community; and to ensure that the lessons learnt from successful schemes are disseminated more widely' (Appendix, para. 3).

1997 also saw the publication of *A Framework for Mental Health Services in Scotland* (Scottish Office, 1997b), heralding the development of 'a joint approach to the planning, commissioning and provision of integrated mental health services' (para. 1). This was the product of extensive consultation and of joint working between the Scottish Office Department of Health, the Social Work Services Group and the Development Department. It was stressed that this did not introduce new policy but focused on ensuring local delivery of a comprehensive mental health service. The framework set out the essential features for a local mental health strategy together with detailed specification of core process and service elements. The interface between primary care, secondary care and social work was addressed in detail. Highlighting the importance of joint planning and working, the framework identified a number of essential components: understanding of and commitment to national and local policies;

involvement of all stakeholders at appropriate levels in planning, delivery and monitoring of services; shared statement of purposes and priorities; a shared assessment of need; an emphasis on implementation; commitment, consistency and co-ordination; clear lead responsibility; clarity about commitment to resources; and clarity about timetable and pathway to implementation (pp. 4–5). Attention is drawn to the publication *Effective Partnerships: Developing Key Indicators for Joint Working in Mental Health* (Sainsbury Centre for Mental Health, 1997) to assist in the monitoring of progress.

Designed to Care and the Mental Health Services Framework signified a much firmer emphasis on the benefits of joint agency working. Post devolution, the first significant statement was *Our National Health: A Plan for Action, a Plan for Change* (Scottish Executive, 2000a), known as the Scottish Health Plan. With an emphasis on 'a shift from the development of policy to the delivery of change', this set out specific initiatives and structural reforms to encourage new forms of partnership between health and social care. The 28 NHS Trusts were to be integrated with the 15 NHS health boards (later reduced to 14) to form unified NHS Boards, with a strong voice for local authorities on these Boards. The Health Improvement Plans and NHS Trust Implementation Plans were to be replaced by a comprehensive Local Health Plan, in turn an integral part of the community plan led by local authorities. 'We want to ensure that the links between the NHS and Local Authorities are strengthened – not just in planning but in service delivery, particularly in community care'(p. 30). There was a particular commitment to meeting the needs of older people, already prefaced as a priority in *A Scotland Where Everyone Matters: Our Visions for Social Justice* (Scottish Executive, 1999), and 40 per cent of both health and social work budgets. 'Effective, integrated services' were called for.

The ideology of partnership, not only with partner agencies but also with staff and with service users, was progressed further in *Partnership for Care: Scotland's Health White Paper* (Scottish Executive, 2003b). The direction of travel is clear.:

> Our focus is on developing services within local communities and strengthening partnerships with Local Authority services. We will achieve this through a massive programme of service redesign, sometimes working across NHS Board boundaries, through partnership working at all levels, and by empowering staff locally to make change happen. (p. 32)

The arrangements for unified NHS Boards and for joint plans were finalised and enacted in the NHS Reform (Scotland) Act 2004. Of particular relevance was the establishment from April 2005 of Community Health Partnerships (CHPs) to replace the LHCCs. These reflected the desire for more local delivery of services, responsive to the needs of the specific community. They were heralded as a whole system service redesign to deliver integrated services and enhanced partnership working. They seek 'to bridge the gap between primary and secondary care and health and social care', enabling better integration of primary health care services with both social work and hospital services. Each CHP was to include the development of a local Public Partnership Forum.

Before moving to the specifics of the Joint Future Agenda, this overview should be completed with the inclusion of *The Same As You?* (Scottish Executive, 2000c), a framework for integrated support for people with learning disabilities that could be considered the Scottish equivalent of *Valuing People*. The key principles of the framework focus on greater inclusion of people with learning disabilities, who would be seen as central to decision making, having greater choice and greater control. Underpinning the recommendations from the review was a clear focus on agencies working together to develop services and support for people with learning disabilities. Two particular initiatives can be highlighted. Local authorities, PCTs and health boards were required by June 2001 to produce 'partnership in practice' agreements (PIPs) covering a three-year period. These were to be a part of, not an addition to, existing planning processes.

> The PIP should draw together the information that is already in existing plans to make sure all the agencies involved in planning services for adults and children with learning disabilities can come to an agreement. (p. 15)

The second initiative was the development of local area co-ordination (Stalker *et al.*, 2007), a model imported from Western Australia whereby a co-ordinator supports perhaps 50 individuals in a local area, providing information and access to support.

Modernising community care

This mapping of the policy development for partnership working between health and social care in Scotland provides a backcloth for the more specific investigation of the community care agenda. *Modernising Community Care: An Action Plan* (Scottish Office, 1998) was published five years after the initial implementation of the relevant sections of the NHS and Community Care Act 1990, and is of particular significance in the evolution of patterns of support provision. The twin aims of the Action Plan were to secure 'better and faster results for people by focusing on them and their needs; and more effective and efficient joint working based on partnership' (p. 2). Directed at local authorities, health boards and trusts, and Scottish Homes, partnership permeates the argument. 'The effectiveness of community care relies on the ability of these organisations to work together and with others to plan and deliver the services people want' (para. 1.3). 'Integrated local partnerships are the way ahead. Joint vision, joint investment and shared responsibility are all vital' (para. 4.0). There was concern to promote the best use of the 'community care pound', and a rejection of any attempt at efficiency savings which merely shunted costs to another agency. In particular the need to progress from strategic plans to the development of comprehensive detailed care and housing strategies for local areas, extending beyond hospital closures, is highlighted. Strategic visions for the future which have measurable targets and timescales need to be specified, together with 'joint strategies, joint plans and joint investments which are then included in community care plans, Health Improvement Plans (HIPs), local authority housing plans and Scottish Homes Regional Plans' (para. 2.5). The recognition of housing as an equal partner is of interest in the light of future emphasis.

Although the option of a single agency is recognised, formal integration is not promoted; the focus is on encouraging joint planning and organisation of services at the local level. The Action Plan advocates what it terms a 'tartan of services' for each area, a range of mechanisms that will promote partnership delivery. Suggestions include the creation of health, housing and social care trusts to pool resources and reduce overheads; staff from different agencies sharing premises; a single manager for community care services; staff to move between agencies; generic workers; pooled or grouped budgets; shared information systems; and joint training. A 'can-do' approach was advocated, with financial leverage offered by way of funds targeted towards shifting the balance of care, developing more flexible home care services, and working in partnership: 'we cannot emphasise strongly enough that joint working across all organisations is one of the most important themes of the new agenda for community care' (p. 7). Responses were sought in respect of barriers in the three areas which have already featured in Chapter Two: pooled budgets, lead commissioning and integrated service provision. The possibility of pooled budgets and lead commissioning with housing interests was also mooted.

A seminar in November 1999 concluded that the ambition of *Modernising Community Care* had not been sufficiently progressed and that new leadership was necessary. In particular there was little evidence of any shift in the balance of care from more institutional settings towards care at home.

The Joint Future initiative

The Joint Future Group was established by the Minister for Health and Community Care in December 1999 as a short-life working group with the aim of finding ways 'to improve joint working in order to deliver modern and effective person-centred services' (Scottish Executive, 2000b, p. 54). It was chaired by the Deputy Minister for Community Care, Iain Gray, and had a core membership of nine key individuals from health and social care. The ambition was to progress the implementation in practice of the principles that had already been highlighted in the earlier Action Plan. Four directives were given to the Group:

- to agree a list of joint measures which agencies need to have in place to deliver effective services, and to set deadlines;
- to advise on the balance between residential and home-based care;
- to advise on options for charging for care at home;
- ˙ to advise on how to identify and share good practice.

A review of existing practice was commissioned from the author of this volume and colleagues to provide some context for the Group on the integration of health and social work service provision. This comprised three phases: an analysis of examples of good practice from the *Community Care Works* database and from Modernising Community Care monitoring returns to the Scottish Executive; three scenario-planning workshops with managers and operational staff to identify barriers and drivers to partnership working and to model future scenarios; and in-depth examination of nine case study examples of joint working. The study was conducted in partnership with an expert witness panel of individuals from health, social work and the voluntary sector. These case studies were:

- Highland: the Howard Doris Centre;
- East Ayrshire: Personal Record of Care;
- Aberdeen: Rapid Response Team;
- Edinburgh: Community Rehabilitation Service;
- East Dunbartonshire: Integrated Occupational Therapy;
- Edinburgh: Mental Health Partnership;
- Angus: Care Management;
- Midlothian: Joint OT (Occupational Therapy) Store;
- South West Glasgow: LHCC.

During the mapping exercise, information on 253 partnership working initiatives was provided by 31 of the 32 local authority areas in Scotland. Conclusions at that date included the following headlines:

- Partnership working was moving forward throughout the country, with a range of models being adopted.
- Joint posts in areas such as commissioning and managing services were seen as an important method of making partnership working a reality and were developing across Scotland.
- Jointly provided services was where partnership working was most well developed.
- Joint access to OT stores and integrated OT services were two emerging areas of development.

In terms of process, the following observations were highlighted. What seemed to work was a focus on outcomes for users rather than a concern with overcoming organisational obstacles; devolving responsibility for budgets to managers of integrated teams; and defining the common purpose around identified need so that people were prepared to set aside their frustrations and stay committed. Traps to avoid included expecting everyone to start in the same place and to work on everything at once; not leaving enough space for creativity; and assuming the lead must always come from statutory services. Still to be learnt, the study suggested, was how to move beyond single initiatives to the re-orientation of mainstream budgets and services; how to put enabling systems behind local communities and not only within organisations; and how to promote and sustain good practice where there is no local champion.

A major outcome from the study was a matrix of barriers and drivers to integrated working (Stewart et al., 2003). These are identified at all levels, from the way that national policy frameworks impact on the local planning context to the operational factors at the front line. The latter are divided into relations between partners, organisational culture, change management, enabling staff, professional behaviour, attitudes and outcomes. A short version of the matrix is presented in Table 3.1, while the full matrix is reproduced in the Appendix.

Lessons for moving forward were summarised as follows:

- All stakeholders need to be involved at the earliest possible stage.

- A shared vision for meeting an agreed need is required in order for progress to be made.

- Individual agency and senior management support needs to be visible.

- Dedicated resources to support change management or development are crucial to moving forward any shared agenda.

- Roles and responsibilities require to be agreed by all stakeholders and need to be clear and unambiguous.

- Joint financial arrangements, pooled or otherwise, should be clear,

- Practical issues are important and can promote ownership and team building; the following issues should be clear in order to reduce the possibility of conflict and loss of focus: location, job description, terms and conditions, workload, appropriate professional supervision.

- Ongoing support to the staff involved on the ground is important to maintain momentum, including joint training.

The Joint Future Group reported in December 2000 (Scottish Executive, 2000b). The key policy messages included local partnership agreements; sharing resources, management and information; joint planning frameworks; accelerated take-up of good practice; and all agencies accountable for

Table 3.1 Drivers and barriers to integrated working (short version) *(Stewart, Petch and Curtice, 2003)*

		Drivers	**Barriers**
A	**National policy frameworks**	joined-up	piecemeal and contradictory
		strategic	promote 'projectitis'
		realistic	unrealistic change agenda
B	**Local planning context**	planning and decision cycles mesh	incompatible planning and decision cycles
		joint acceptance of unmet need	not needs led
		agreed, comprehensive vision, owned at all levels	issues seen in isolation
C	**Operational factors**		
	Relations between partners	trust permits risk-taking	lack of trust prevents risk-taking
		open, honest communication	defensive, limited communication
	Organisational culture	'can do' culture	sees institutional and legal barriers
		collective responsibility publicly demonstrated	senior figures devalue/disown common purpose
	Change management	flexible enough to learn as goes	presses on regardless
	Enabling staff	agreed roles and responsibilities	unclear responsibilities, conflict
		staff valued	staff expendable
	Professional behaviour	centred on user need	tribal, protectionist
		willing to take risks	covers own back
	Attitudes	'we have nothing to lose'	'we have everything to lose'
		'we will find a way'	'no way'
	Outcomes	user focused	only seen from agencies' agenda
		visible	invisible
		benefits shared	winners and losers

performance. The nineteen recommendations, grouped into five core areas, were designed to deliver a 'step change'.

Rebalancing care of older people has long been a central tenet of community care policy. The Joint Future Group identified five key developments which it wished to see. These ranged from basic domestic support services to short breaks and rapid response and augmented care schemes (Scottish Executive, 2000b, paras 2.1–2.5):

- Every local authority area should have in place a comprehensive, joint hospital discharge/rapid response team, by mid 2001–02.

- Every local authority area should have in place a comprehensive, joint intensive home support team, by mid 2001–02.

- Each year, agencies should provide both more short breaks (to reduce the number of carers providing most care, without a break), and more breaks at home.

- Every local authority should identify the need for a practical shopping/domestic/household service, and arrange it comprehensively by mid 2001–02.

- The Executive should, in 2001, set up an older people's service development centre to champion the development of good and innovative community care services, promote training and assist implementation of the Group's proposals.

Improving joint working was to be facilitated by five key elements: single assessments, intensive care management, information sharing, equipment and adaptations, and OT services. These were identified in the following recommendations (paras 2.6–2.13):

- Agencies locally should have in place single, shared assessment procedures for older people and for those with dementia by October 2001, and for all client groups by April 2002.

- Agencies locally should have in place by October 2001, a single shared assessment tool for older people and people with dementia. Local agencies should either adapt existing systems or develop systems to achieve the outcomes specified in the report, or adopt Carenap D and E.

- The Scottish Executive should redefine care management as Intensive Care Management, which will be for people with complex or frequently changing needs.

- Care managers should be trained in Intensive Care Management throughout 2001–2002. Only those who have undertaken such training should carry out Intensive Care Management.

- The Scottish Executive should, by 2002, offer a strategic lead on the development of community care information, information sharing and systems integration.

- Locally, the arrangements for single shared assessments should include specific proposals for the necessary sharing of information between agencies, by obtaining explicit client approval.

- To modernise and improve equipment and adaptation services, the Scottish Executive should establish a strategic overview, and set out a programme of change that will require agencies locally to integrate equipment and adaptation services with the rest of community care services, and put in place a number of specific measures that will result in a better-focused and more effective service for the user.

- To target occupational therapy services more effectively, agencies need to modernise equipment and adaptation services, and to remove duplication between hospital and community based occupational therapy services wherever practical. For community care services that reorganisation needs to begin as soon as possible, followed by the rest of health and social care within the context of the wider agenda for joined up health, housing and social care services.

Planning, financial and service management frameworks with specific features were to be developed. At the macro level there was to be a national planning and financial framework; at the local level, joint resourcing and joint service management was to be introduced (paras 2.14–2.16):

- The Scottish Executive should set up a programme planning and financial framework, beginning with services for older people in 2001.

- Local authorities (that is social work and housing), health boards, NHS trusts and Scottish Homes should draw up local partnership agreements, including a clear programme for local joint resourcing and joint management of community care services collectively or for each care user group individually.

- As a step towards that, and recognising current progress on the ground, every area should introduce joint resourcing and joint management of services for older people from April 2002, and in preparation for that introduce shadow arrangements in the course of 2001–02.

Charging, and in particular the diversity of practice across different authorities, had long been a focus for debate. The Joint Future Group identified two key areas for recommendation (paras 2.17–2.18):

- COSLA should develop guidance on charging policies to reduce the inconsistencies in home care charging.

- The Scottish Executive should consider introducing:
  - free home care for up to 4 weeks for older people leaving hospital;
  - free home care for older people receiving extended home care (though they would still pay for ordinary services).

The final recommendation of the Group related to *good practice* (para. 2.19):

- The Scottish Executive should, by mid 2001–02, identify measures to improve the collection and dissemination of good practice by linking together the bodies in the field in a more cohesive structure, using the benefits of networking and information technology.

The Scottish Executive published a response to *Community Care: A Joint Future* in January 2001 (Scottish Executive, 2001a). All the recommendations were endorsed, save for that relating to free home care for older people receiving extended home care. This was referred to a Development Group on Long Term Care. This was to be chaired by Malcolm Chisholm in preparation for the progression of a Long Term Care Bill. Subsequently, the remit of this group was focused on taking forward the implementation of free personal care following the decision of the Scottish Parliament in January 2001 (Care Development Group, 2001).

Meanwhile the Scottish Executive had already issued a Statement on Older People in October 2000 (Scottish Executive, 2000d). This set out a number of key developments and was heralded as a 'step change in care to older people in Scotland'. The specific features included:

- the development of rapid response teams for every locality providing fast and flexible support;
- the development of intensive home support/augmented home care schemes;
- the provision of 22,000 additional weeks of respite care;
- the development of services designed to provide practical assistance with shopping, domestic and household maintenance tasks;
- the introduction of joint resourcing and service management by 2002;
- the provision of free home care for up to four weeks on leaving hospital;
- the provision of further equipment and adaptations;
- an allocation of an annual sum of £10 million to tackle delayed discharge.

The first six features accord with recommendations 1–4, 16 and 18 of the Joint Future Group report. Additional finance was committed to the value of £30 million in 2001 and £36 million in 2002. To take forward the recommendations from the report of the Joint Future Group, the former Community Care Implementation Unit was transformed into the Joint Future Unit.

The introduction of rapid response teams had been triggered by the success of a number of high profile pilots. In South Ayrshire, for example, a rapid response team with eight core staff had focused on providing support to individuals who could be supported at home with a multidisciplinary integrated package of care. The service was for those whose need for such support was short term, ideally less than 14 days; it was not designed for individuals with long-term or deteriorating conditions. Over the three-month initial period they worked with 188 people, supporting early discharge for 118 and avoiding the need for hospital admission for 70.

In Angus, a supported discharge scheme had offered intensive community-based care for older people. This was targeted at people who were deemed vulnerable on grounds of living alone or with an older partner or relative as the main carer; at those who were frail or had experienced a significant reduction in functional abilities as a result of hospitalisation; and at those in need of emotional or psychological support during readjustment. The named nurse in the hospital referred the individual to the care co-ordinator, who designed a support package which could last from one to six weeks, providing weekly support between 7 a.m. and 11 p.m. with up to two overnights. Such schemes were perceived as key in advancing the priority of enabling more people to be supported within their own homes and in fostering the necessary co-ordination across different professional groups and agencies.

The relevant sections of the Community Care and Health (Scotland) Act 2002 can be highlighted here, before moving in the next chapter to an examination of the detailed implementation of the Joint Future Agenda. The Act took forward a number of the policy commitments referenced above, including the responses from the Scottish Executive to the reports from the Royal Commission on Long Term Care (October 2000), the Health and Community Care Committee's Inquiry into the Delivery of Community Care (Scottish Parliament, 2000) and the Joint Future Group (January 2001). Part Two enacts measures similar to the 1999 Health Act flexibilities in England. Section 13 allows payments from the NHS towards certain local authority functions; Section 14 covers the reciprocal arrangement for payment from local authorities towards NHS functions. Section 15 addresses pooled budgets and lead provision, while Section 17 allows Ministers to enforce joint working arrangements if it is deemed that adequate progress has not been made and services are failing. These changes, along with others addressed in the Act, were trailed in a consultation paper issued in April 2001, *Better Care for All Our Futures* (Scottish Executive, 2001b), and the detailed implementation is specified in a guidance circular, CCD 11/2002.

It is appropriate to note at this stage two major areas that are notable for their absence from the Joint Future evolution. The first is the role of housing, long championed as the cornerstone of community care but apparently no longer core to the debate. The second is the role of the voluntary sector. In England the silence over its contribution in the debate on partnership working has been traced by Wyatt (2002). In Scotland it was left to Community Care Providers Scotland to draw attention to the omission of their sector in a report in 2002, *A Joint Future for Community Care: A Voluntary Sector Perspective* (Community Care Providers Scotland, 2002):

Despite the importance of the voluntary sector service providers in relation to community care in Scotland, the national policy debate on joint working has almost entirely ignored the sector, its services and its expertise. (p. 3)

CHAPTER 4

Initial Joint Future Strategies

I think on the whole they worked extremely well together. They
pass messages onto each other. They leave a book, each one
writes notes on what they've done for the next one who comes
and they can see what has been done.

The Joint Future report had set an ambitious agenda, with the potential to place partnership working and the delivery of integrated services at the heart of support for individuals with particular needs. This chapter will examine the initial areas which were targeted – single shared assessment and Local Partnership Agreements – and track the progress towards achieving the goals of the Agenda.

Single shared assessment

The process of assessment is at the heart of the provision of support: however, the drivers behind assessment have varied over the years. Prior to the development of the community care systems set out in the 1990 NHS and Community Care Act, individuals would be allocated to services on the basis of crude criteria such as age or impairment. The Audit Commission report (1986) *Making a Reality of Community Care*, the precursor to the White Paper *Caring for People* and the 1990 Act, identified the lack of appropriate assessment procedures as one of a number of fundamental structural problems in the existing system. Assessment procedures were service-led and lacked flexibility, with little attempt to identify or respond to the particular needs of individuals. The lack of needs assessment had also led to the exponential rise in care home placements through individuals accessing the DHSS residential care allowance. The subsequent legislation introduced the requirement for a community care assessment, identifying the particular needs of an individual and determining the appropriate response.

Circular SSWG 11/91 in Scotland was the first circular to offer comprehensive guidance detailing the key features of the assessment (and care management) process. It was to be needs-led, not service-led; use an initial screening process; ensure the participation of the individual and any informal carer; embrace physical, mental and social functioning; make a clear decision as to the services required; detail the conclusions, the review procedures, and the name of a contact person; and provide information about the complaints procedure. A subsequent circular, SWSG 10/98, *Community Care Needs of Frail People: Integrating Professional Assessments and Care Arrangements*, focused specifically on older people. The initial development of the community care assessment process has been widely debated (by, for example, Nolan and Caldock, 1996; Ellis *et al.*, 1999), and has received detailed scrutiny in Scotland (Petch *et al.*, 1996).

Much of the initial focus of the assessment process centred on the development of the assessment tool, a somewhat elusive search for an ideal. There was also, however, the need for a cultural shift amongst those conducting assessments, a switch from the tradition of 'this person requires a day centre' to 'this person has a need for support and activity during the day'. With the advent of joint working a new perspective on assessment emerged, an early concern about the extent to which individuals were subject to multiple assessments from different professionals. As a result, rapid introduction of a single shared assessment process (SSA) was one of the key targets set by the Joint Future Group.

Circular CCD8/2001 marked the shift in policy towards the SSA, recognising 'the lead responsibility of social work within local authorities but also that effective partnerships and engagement of both health and housing professionals are essential to achieve the holistic approach that Ministers want'. SSA would be 'person-centred, more streamlined, led by a single professional, with other specialist involvement as appropriate, and the results would be acceptable to all professionals in social work, health and housing' (p. 8). A number of requirements were identified:

- the development of a new culture for assessment, placing the needs of the individual as paramount;

- a more holistic and efficient approach to assessment;

- a broader range of assessors, including health and housing professionals;

- the use of local assessment tools meeting a set of minimum standards or the use of Carenap D or E (McWalter *et al.*, 1994);

- collective ownership of the new arrangements.

Table 4.1 below, reproduced from the guidance, highlights the benefits that it was argued would result for both service users and agencies. The importance, however, of advancing parallel development in joint resourcing and joint management (see below) is stressed.

The balance between local discretion and central control is epitomised in the debates that have ensued as to whether a common assessment tool should be imposed for the conduct of the SSA or whether different localities should be able to develop their own tools. A baseline set of minimum standards expected to be met by locally developed tools was defined. These specified

Table 4.1 Expected benefits from Single Shared Assessment *(Circular CCD 8/2001)*

Benefits for people who use services	Benefits for agencies
• focuses on their needs and those of their carers	• minimises duplication of work
• offers an appropriate level and range of assessment	• reduces bureaucracy
• avoids duplication of information-giving, and a number of assessments	• integrates systems and procedures
• provides a key contact person (i.e. the lead assessor)	• achieves better use of staff skills and expertise
• achieves speedier and integrated care planning	• makes more effective use of resources
• provides access to a range of co-ordinated services	• supports and builds on good practice
	• results accepted by fellow professionals

the detail of the assessment process and of the assessment tool, and, for older people only, a core data set. Alternatively there was the option, for older people, of adopting the Care Needs Assessment Package for the Elderly (Carenap E) (and for dementia, Carenap D). This had been developed as a multidisciplinary tool, with needs recorded as 'no need', 'met need' or 'unmet need'. Accompanying software allowed the aggregation of individual unmet need to determine need at the community level. The importance of developing integrated information systems was also stressed.

Circular CCD8/2001 also introduced the prospect of the Resource Use Measure (RUM). The initial motivation for this measure was to standardise the translation of the outcome of an assessment into the level of resource necessary to meet the identified needs. Practically this would allow eligibility for free nursing or personal care to be determined; longer term the aspiration was to ensure greater equity in provision for a given level of need. It was anticipated that the completion of the RUM would be based on the SSA and would add only a few minutes to the initial assessment. The initial ambition was to apply a single RUM across Scotland from April 2002.

The development of the RUM from the initial adaptation of two earlier measures (SCRUGS – the Scottish Care Resource Utilisation Groups – and Isaacs and Neville's Intervals of Need) can be traced through a series of pilot and development stages (Scottish Executive, 2002a). Initially developed in five case study areas, the single measure was subsequently piloted in nine initial areas and then developed across a further 29 sites. Circular CCD9/2002 in September 2002 confirmed the requirement for all partnership areas across Scotland to use the RUM to inform their planning process from April 2003. Five partnership areas started the process from January 2003.

Subsequently the focus of the RUM shifted from its association with determining entitlement to free personal and nursing care: 'the purpose changed from a measure of resource use to a standardised measure of relative need' (Circular CCD5/2004, para. 3). From April 2004 it was rebranded as the Single Shared Assessment Indicator of Relative Need (SSA-IoRN) and was to be extended from the initial five partnership sites to the whole of Scotland, rolled out between 2004 and 2006. It applies only to people over 65. The guidance circular CCD5/2004 provides extensive detail of the lengthy development process. The operational guidance comprises two elements, a user handbook for frontline practitioners and a resource pack on CD-ROM for strategic managers on roll-out plans.

In its developed form the SSA-IoRN comprises 12 questions addressing five core areas: ADL(Activities of Daily Living)/mobility; personal care; food and drink preparation; mental well-being and behaviour; and bowel management. Responses are drawn from the information already gathered for the SSA. On the basis of the responses, individuals are classified into one of nine groups (ranging from A, low need to I, high need) according to their relative level of need. Four elements were identified as key in promoting the implementation of the SSA-IoRN: co-located/integrated teams; meeting Joint Future Agenda aims and objectives; good leadership; and good support frameworks both locally and nationally. Associated with the initial development was the RUM-ICADS – an Integrated Care Assessment Data Summary. This continues to be developed, relabelled as the Care Assessment Data Summary.

The extent to which strategies have been developed for gathering the perspectives of users and carers on the SSA process has been explored by the Infusion Co-operative (2005). This aimed to map developing practice across Scotland and to develop a toolkit for measuring user and carer satisfaction with SSA. The review suggested that a culture of seeking users' and carers' views, particularly those of older people, is well established. With regard to SSA, responses revealed a gap between what professionals saw as a priority for the process and what individuals saw as priorities in their lives. The need to use a range of techniques and to appreciate the different strengths and weaknesses of different methods was highlighted. A particular focus was on strategies to overcome communication difficulties, with an encouraging range of initiatives.

An interesting perspective on the SSA is presented by Ferguson (2003). The emphasis on partnership working in general and the promotion of the SSA in particular is, he argues, a classic example of managerialism. The likelihood of users benefiting as a result of the SSA process is uncertain: the role of assessment as a basis for rationing scarce resources needs to be acknowledged, while greater integration may reduce bureaucracy but does not necessarily empower the individual service user. Ferguson also suggests that SSA is likely to reflect and enhance traditional status variations between different professional groups, and to perpetuate the market discourse of choice.

Local Partnership Agreements

The second key focus from the Joint Future Group was the emphasis on joint resourcing and joint management. In order to achieve the April 2002 target from the original report, guidance was issued in September 2001 in the form of Circular CCD7/2001. This built on a range of statements which had prefaced the concept, including the response in October 2000 to the Royal Commission on Long Term Care (Scottish Executive, 2000e) and the Scottish Health Plan, *Our National Health: A Plan for Action, a Plan for Change*, of December 2000. As outlined in Chapter Three, any legislative barriers were to be tackled in the Community Care and Health (Scotland) Act 2002, together with the introduction of powers to intervene, if required, to compel agencies to work together.

The guidance listed a number of arguments in favour of joint resourcing and joint management from the perspective of service users (para. 6). These included the facility to:

- promote early assessment and intervention;
- remove barriers within the individual's care journey, and have a positive impact on care outcomes and the number of patients waiting for discharge;
- provide more consistent and integrated services in localities;
- create more single points of access to community care services;
- strengthen locality working and the deployment of resources closer to users', patients' and carers' needs, leading to greater flexibility and responsiveness of services.

Arguments were also presented for the benefits to a range of other stakeholders. For example, it would enable elected and appointed members to take decisions across the wider resource base, developing a more whole-person approach, while front-line practitioners would be able to engage with a wider skill base.

Six key 'action steps' were outlined in the circular; these were to be based on the partnership's vision of the services they wanted to develop and commission for older people over the next five years (para. 9). The steps were:

- agreement on joint management arrangements;
- agreement on the resources (including staff, money, equipment and property) to be brought under joint management arrangements;
- agreement on outline joint development priorities and the associated organisational and people development plans and targets for the next three to five years;
- agreement on joint governance and accountability arrangements;
- agreement on the joint performance management framework;
- production of a Local Partnership Agreement (LPA) by 1 April 2002.

The expectation was that the features in the LPAs would then become part of the existing planning mechanisms including community plans, local health plans, community care plans and local housing strategies.

Detail was provided for each of the six steps. For example, three potential models for joint management, bringing together NHS and local authority resources (staff, money, equipment and property), were identified. The first model outlined a joint management structure where there are aligned budgets, a joint committee or board and a joint senior management group. Under the second model, a partnership body is set up bringing together staff, equipment and property with aligned budgets (Partnership Body Type A). The Care Together initiative in Perth and Kinross was the first example of this type. It was envisaged that under this model there would be clearer delegated responsibilities and decision making, a clearer identity, and a high level single manager. Neither of these models constitutes a legal entity and therefore staff remain employed by the individual agencies.

In the third model (Partnership Body Type B), the budgets for the partnership body were to be pooled, with the expectation that this would give greater flexibility. A high level manager would have responsibility across the range of health, social care and housing services. There would still be a requirement for one of the bodies to act as host for the pooled budget, and the partnership body would not be able to employ staff, requiring that staff were either employed by or seconded to the host agency.

The circular also detailed the range of items that should be included in the joint resourcing pot for older people. This was to include local authority social work services and budgets for older people; health, social work and housing equipment and adaptation services; Supporting People funding; dedicated NHS services for older people such as continuing care, assessment and rehabilitation services, day hospitals, and services commissioned from the independent sector; health visitors and district nurses; and relevant aspects of acute services.

Conflicts in terms and conditions between staff from different professional groups are often presented as some of the most intractable barriers to partnership working. Yet as exemplified in the barriers and drivers matrix, they can be transcended by those who are determined to make progress. An Integrated Human Resource Working Group was established to take forward the recommendations from the Joint Future Group relating to the workforce and to design a joint staffing framework.

The working group's report (Scottish Executive, 2002b) acknowledged the anxieties generated around different NHS and local authority procedures and conditions, and clarified that for the medium term the framework should assume that staff will continue to be employed by their existing organisation. Consultation with the workforce had identified a number of 'critical requirements'. These included the development of trust, an ethos of honesty, recognition of professionalism, a joint approach to changing cultures, consistent and clear communication, and a regular exchange of knowledge. A raft of recommendations was presented addressing specifics of the human resources agenda. These included the development of local Joint Future staff fora alongside the national staffing framework; a planned approach to change; the production of joint Organisation Development and Training Plans; local joint training; inter-professional education and training; and the enhancement of both skills and multidisciplinary competencies. It was recommended that the harmonisation of terms and conditions should in the medium term be negotiated locally, somewhat of a disappointment to those who had hoped the working group would propose a national solution for this often intractable challenge.

Early progress

The Joint Future Agenda presented a radical change agenda. The early years of the Agenda were characterised by shifting deadlines and variable progress. A letter was issued to partnership agencies by the Scottish Executive on 3 January 2002 setting out the 'bottom line' in terms of progressing both SSA and joint resourcing and management. It was acknowledged that there was a 'crowded agenda' with a number of areas to progress. Partnerships were to agree an implementation plan by April 2002, with the expectation that full implementation in the two areas would be achieved by April 2003.

A further letter on 8 March 2002 detailed the requirements. In respect of joint resourcing and joint management, partnerships were required as a minimum to include in their initial Local Partnership Agreement for April 2002 the first two of the six action steps specified in CCD7/2001 and outlined above; to have progressed the human resources agenda; and to have developed an action plan on how they would be achieving full implementation by April 2003. Of particular importance to the 'bottom line' was to scope the total joint resource 'pot' and to identify what was to be included at the beginning, particularly in respect of older people's services. Detail and timescales were also required for the joint management arrangements to be adopted, both joint committees or partnership bodies and single manager posts. Partnerships were asked to specify their intentions in terms of pooled or aligned budgets and to indicate whether any functions were to be delegated. Details were also to be provided of the joint staff forum and of joint training and organisational development plans.

For SSA, the 'bottom line' requirement was to have the structures in place for older people's services by April 2002 and for the full range of service user groups a year later. For 2002, therefore, there was to be agreement for older people on:

- single shared assessment systems and procedures;
- an assessment tool and how it was to be used;

- a protocol for sharing information and for securing the assessed person's consent;

- a plan to fully implement single shared assessment both for older people and for the rest of community care by April 2003.

By the following year, however, timescales had slipped again. In February 2003 a 'next steps' letter was issued by the three parties, the Scottish Executive, NHS Scotland and COSLA, in which it was acknowledged that 'some difficulties have been experienced in certain areas'. In August 2002 a 'summit meeting' of Ministers, council leaders and NHS chairs had met. The commitment to the Joint Future Agenda had been confirmed. A Ministerial Steering Group was to lead the Agenda, with a high level policy group, the Joint Future Implementation and Advisory Group (JFIAG) to plan and monitor the implementation. The JFIAG was to be chaired jointly by the Chief Executive of NHSScotland and the Chief Executive of COSLA, symbolising the priority attached to this area. It met for the first time in January 2003 and agreed the following remit:

- provide clear national direction and impetus;
- facilitate user and carer involvement;
- generate consensus on joint services;
- promote local development and implementation;
- provide signposting and guidance;
- promote consistency, equity and quality;
- monitor delivery of the policy.

The minutes of both these groups can be accessed on the Scottish Executive Joint Future website (www.scotland.gov.uk/Topics/health/care/Joint-Future), providing an accessible snapshot of the progress of the different strands and initiatives.

The 'next steps' letter emanated from the JFIAG. It serves both as a summary of progress at that stage and as an announcement of further revision in timescales. For example, joint resourcing and joint management was now to be implemented for older people's services by April 2003, but for other groups the expectation was delayed until April 2004, although the JFIAG considered that 'mental health, learning disability and drugs misuse services are well placed to make an early transition into the joint arrangements'. Similarly, the letter indicated that implementation of SSA was to be phased over 2003 and 2004. Specifically the expectation was for:

- SSA for all older people by April 2003;
- arrangements for information sharing to support SSA by April 2003;
- agreement on how the SSA tools and processes would be applied to other community care groups by April 2003; with
- SSA in place for all other groups by April 2004;

- all local partnerships to introduce the RUM by the end of 2003–4.

The hope was that if satisfactory arrangements for both SSA and joint resourcing and joint management could be established for older people's services, 'local partnerships should be able to move quickly to extend the Joint Future Agenda to other community care groups'.

The 'next steps' letter also signalled the growing shift towards a more outcome-led focus – 'this letter moves beyond the initial focus on structures and processes towards developing joint services and improved outcomes for people who use services, across the community care spectrum'. For example, Local Outcome Agreements had been proposed in respect of the October 2000 funding package for home care services outlined above. A requirement was introduced that Local Outcome Agreements for services to older people were to be agreed between the Joint Future Unit and local authorities by April 2003.

Involvement of service users and carers is of course a theme that runs throughout the development of adult support services. 'Next steps', however, raised the priority for such involvement within the Joint Future Agenda by introducing an expectation that 'local partnerships will ensure effective means of involving patients, service users and carers in the Joint Future Agenda'. It was expected that voluntary organisations would contribute to achieving this goal, both as representative groups and as advocacy organisations. Independent sector providers, both voluntary and private, were also expected to be embraced within the implementation of the Agenda: 'local partnerships should develop effective mechanisms to involve the independent sector in the Joint Future Agenda'.

Joint Performance Information and Assessment Framework

By 2003 the Joint Future Agenda had evolved to a stage at which thoughts turned to the need to assess to what extent the partnerships were performing against the desired objectives. Performance indicators current at that point related to measurement from a single agency perspective: Circular CCD1/2003 introduced a new Joint Performance Information and Assessment Framework (JPIAF), which sought measures that would reflect the joined-up policy agenda:

> The Joint Future Agenda exemplifies community planning in action at a local level. Joint resourcing and joint management provide the local structures for effective partnership working in one area – community care services – and the JPIAF performance indicators focus on joint actions within the Joint Future Agenda. Joint Future and community planning are therefore pursuing the same kinds of goal, but at different levels. (Annex A, para. 5)

The new framework was developed following a consultation process during which the preference for focusing on a relatively small number of meaningful indicators had been emphasised. The JPIAF focused initially on two key elements of the Joint Future Agenda: joint resourcing and joint management, and single shared assessment. These initial indicators focused primarily on process and were based on the four key aims for the Joint Future Agenda:

- better outcomes for people who use community care services and their carers;
- better use of resources, both health and local authority;
- better management of services and more service re-design leading to more joint services;
- better systems with less bureaucracy and duplication.

The framework itself had the following key characteristics:

- an integrated matrix approach, using both statistical performance indicators and those being developed around quality of services;
- national key joint performance indicators, using or adapting wherever possible existing performance indicators;
- national joint performance assessment arrangements for data collection, analysis and reporting, undertaken by Audit Scotland, Social Work Services Inspectorate (SWSI) and the Joint Future Unit;
- strengthening local joint responsibility or accountability mechanisms for joint working.

This initial formulation identified nine JPIAF indicators. The first three related to joint management arrangements: JPIAF 1 focused on joint management arrangements, JPIAF 2 on joint governance and accountability arrangements, and JPIAF 3 on joint action on human resource issues.

JPIAF 4 related to joint resourcing, specifically the joint financial framework as part of the full Local Partnership Agreement, and refers back to the initial Circular, CCD7/2001, and to the subsequent requirements (as described under 'Local Partnership Agreements' above) to have effective joint resourcing arrangements in place for older people's services by April 2003 and for other groups by April 2004. Circular 7/2001 had detailed the options for pooled or aligned budgets. All local partnerships indicated that they intended to adopt aligned budgets at April 2003.

Five indicators (JPIAF 5 to JPIAF 9) were to focus on single shared assessment, building on the features outlined above (under 'Single shared assessment') from the original Circular 8/2001 on Single Shared Assessment of Community Care Needs. JPIAF 5 addressed the implementation of the single shared assessment framework, both for older people and for other groups; JPIAF 6 was to focus on speedier assessments; JPIAF 7 referred to joint training for SSA; JPIAF 8 identified the use of joint protocols for accessing resources; and JPIAF 9 the use of joint information-sharing protocols.

All JPIAF indicator returns were to be analysed as part of the Annual Statement for each of the 32 local partnerships to be prepared by Audit Scotland, SWSI and the Joint Future Unit. It was recognised that these initial indicators focused primarily on process, with the promise of more outcome-focused measures in subsequent years.

An initial assessment in July 2003 of the progress of partnerships against the nine JPIAF indicators reported 'good progress had been made by the majority of local partnerships in relation to most of the JPIAF indicators'. Across the indicators as a whole:

- 4 of the 32 partnerships met or were close to meeting all of the JPIAF indicators;

- 14 were well progressed;

- 12 were still being progressed; and

- 2 were insufficiently progressed or lacked sufficient evidence.

Equipment, adaptations and joint premises

The 'next steps' letter also highlighted the Strategy Forum on Equipment and Adaptations, charged in response to the directive in the Joint Future report with establishing a sense of direction for equipment and adaptation services. The Forum's report, *Equipped for Inclusion*, was issued in June 2003, with an invitation for responses to its 35 recommendations. An accompanying publication, *Using the Law to Develop and Improve Equipment and Adaptation Provision* (Scottish Executive, 2003e), seeks to clarify the legal requirements and safeguards.

Four key areas were identified as essential to achieving a strategic vision. Firstly, equipment and adaptations should be seen as part of everyday life. Secondly, extending and sharing knowledge is critical; improvements are needed both in the availability of information and in how it is provided. Thirdly, equipment and adaptations have to be integral to a joint future through inclusion in joint resourcing and joint service management, in single shared assessment, and in care management. Finally, assuring quality and innovation is essential:

> The Joint Future Agenda provides mechanisms that offer an unparalleled opportunity to overcome the gaps, overlaps and unhelpful demarcations that hinder delivery of equipment and adaptation services. (Scottish Executive, 2003a, p. 2)

Another area tackled in the wake of the Joint Future report was joint premises. A short-life working group on Joint Premises in Primary and Community Care produced its final report in July 2003 (Scottish Executive, 2003d). The ambition was to remove obstacles that inhibited integrated approaches to the funding and management of joint premises, and to provide a generic toolkit to assist local partners in progressing developments. Dalmellington Area Centre and the Strathbrock Partnership Centre in Broxburn, West Lothian were commended as flagship developments. The Joint Premises report highlights the further imperative for partnership working in the community planning requirements of the Local Government in Scotland Act 2003. Local authorities are charged with facilitating the community planning process, and health and other agencies with participating in it. In this context the Joint Future Agenda is referred to as 'community planning in action'.

CHAPTER 5

From Process to Outcome:
The Current Joint Future Agenda

One phone call for all, if you get my meaning ... as opposed to
a phone book full of separate numbers.

In Chapter Four the initial years of the Joint Future Agenda were explored. The emphasis in these initial years had inevitably been on developing the process of partnership working, and on developing the infrastructures which it was thought would facilitate more integrated working. In this chapter the more recent shift to an outcomes focus will be explored, highlighting the later priorities of the Joint Future Agenda. At the same time as progressing outcomes, the need for a more integrated approach with other developments such as Community Health Partnerships, delayed discharges and community planning was highlighted.

Local Improvement Targets

The shift in emphasis was most clearly signalled by the commitment of Tom McCabe, Deputy Minister for Health and Local Government at the time, to 're-invigorate the Joint Future Agenda'. The continuing revision of target dates and the high profile of other initiatives such as the introduction of free personal care for older people had led some to a sense that the Joint Future Agenda had stalled. In March 2004 a paper was published outlining a framework of four key national outcomes for service users and carers which should be the objective for partnership activity. The four outcomes were as follows:

- Supporting more people at home, as an alternative to residential and nursing care, where it is appropriate. This involves better access to a range of care services, whether health, housing or social care, in their own homes.
- Assisting people to lead independent lives through reducing inappropriate admission to hospital, reducing time spent inappropriately in hospital and enabling supported and faster transfers from hospital.
- Ensuring people receive an improved quality of care through faster access to services and better quality services.

- Better involvement of and support for carers.

Within the context of these four national outcomes, each local partnership was expected to set Local Improvement Targets detailing how they would be addressed. Such targets were expected to conform to SMART principles – i.e. specific, measurable, achievable, relevant and time-bound.

Circular CCD9/2004, issued in July 2004, detailed for each of the four national outcomes a number of core areas for which partnerships are asked to identify Local Improvement Targets. For example, in respect of supporting more people at home, partnerships were asked to identify increasing use of intensive home care (defined as over ten hours per week) and improved access to equipment and adaptation services. Appropriate targets might be to increase by 10 per cent each year the number of intensive home care packages, or to reduce by 5 per cent by a specific date the number of people waiting for equipment, maintaining an approach of continuous improvement. Likewise, for carers the targets set are an increase in receiving short breaks and an increase in the total number of hours of respite. Overall across the four outcomes, 12 core areas for Local Improvement Targets were identified. The local detail had to be specified for the first time in the Extended Local Partnership Agreements to be produced in 2004.

Extended Local Partnership Agreements

The initial focus for the implementation of the Joint Future Agenda was older people. The release of Circular CCD2/2004 in February 2004 (Extended Local Partnership Agreements and the Joint Performance Information and Assessment Framework) extended the scope of the Agenda across the range of community care services. Extended Local Partnership Agreements (ELPAs) were to be submitted by 30 April 2004, reporting the progress that had been made; at the same time there were adjustments to the JPIAF for this second year as part of the drive for continuous improvement.

The circular discussed features specific to particular groups, for example the Partnership in Practice agreements for individuals with learning disabilities detailed in *The Same as You?* The Scottish Executive acknowledged that as well as providing the detail for the ELPAs, local partnerships were also involved in the development of Community Health Partnerships (CHPs) and in the production of delayed discharge plans. Schemes of establishment for CHPs were to be submitted later in 2004 (indeed some had argued for harmonisation of the dates) and partnerships were asked to cross reference to both the planned CHPs and their delayed discharge plans. Cross reference to developments under Supporting People was also encouraged.

The creation of Community Health Partnerships, heralded in *Partnership for Care* and *Delivering for Health*, is an interesting development in the context of the Joint Future Agenda. The Community Health Partnerships Statutory Guidance issued in October 2004 clearly states the intention that the CHPs work in partnership with local authorities as the local focus for implementing the agenda, with health boards devolving authority to the CHPs:

> We expect local partners to continue to support and accelerate the development of Joint Future as a key component of the development of CHPs so as to maintain momentum in serving their communities and delivering better outcomes from care delivered locally. (para. 34)

The guidance argued that the infrastructure for joint working was firmly established and that it should be the basis for the evolution of CHPs as the partner with local authorities for Local Outcome Agreements and Delayed Discharge Action Plans as well as the ELPAs highlighted above. Despite these assertions, there was considerable feeling at the time that CHPs were being proposed and developed from somewhat of a silo position, proceeding on a parallel rather than integrated track from the Joint Future Agenda. It is worthy of note that subsequently Glasgow has decided to develop five integrated Community Health and Care Partnerships.

In respect of the JPIAF there were a number of modifications from the initial year. JPIAF 9 on the joint protocol for information sharing was discontinued as most partnerships had a protocol in place. JPIAF 6 on the number of single shared assessments was to be modified as it had emerged that returns had used inconsistent definitions; a subsequent circular in June (CCD7/2004) clarified the process that was to constitute a 'single shared assessment'. The other SSA indicators (5, 7, 8 and 9) remained as before, but reporting for all community care groups.

Two new performance indicators were specified. JPIAF 10 introduced an attempt at a whole system indicator, seeking to capture whole system working in respect of a key area, the balance of care. The aim was to assemble the indicator from existing data, charting the number of people receiving a single shared assessment; the number of delayed discharges; the number of individuals over 65 admitted to hospital as an emergency; the number supported long term in accommodation other than their own home; and the number of individuals supported in their own home through the provision of ten or more hours of home care. JPIAF 11 was described as a local joint performance assessment framework indicator and sought information on outputs or outcomes for individuals/carers/groups which partnerships had been able to assess locally. For 2004 all indicators apart from JPIAF 10 applied to the whole of community care rather than just older people as in 2003. Following the submission of the ELPAs, the Scottish Executive was to prepare annual evaluation statements during May and June. Local partnerships were to respond by July and the statements together with a national overview would be published at the end of July 2004. The agreed Annual Evaluation Statements for each partnership are published annually on the Joint Future

Unit website. These give an appraisal for progress on each JPIAF indicator and an overall assessment.

Joint Improvement Team

The Joint Improvement Team (JIT) was established in 2004 following a proposal from the Joint Future Implementation and Advisory Group. It carries the strap-line 'supporting health and social care partnerships'. The ambition was that a specialist team would be able to work with health and social care partnerships to accelerate the delivery of service improvements for service users and carers. The team is itself a partnership body, sponsored by the Scottish Executive, NHSScotland and COSLA (Convention of Scottish Local Authorities). It has four strands of work: an intensive support programme, shared learning, an information and advice service, and policy and development – progressing key issues facing partnerships and identifying opportunities to support continuous improvement. The intention is that involvement with partnerships in the intensive support programme is on a voluntary basis, offering practical support and additional capacity to focus on key aspects of service delivery over a period of up to twelve months.

In an information leaflet issued in 2005, the JIT introduces itself thus:

> The JIT will provide a range of information, advice and support to health and social care partnerships, and will encourage and facilitate shared learning and good practice. It will adopt a solutions-based approach that seeks positive outcomes through supportive programmes. It will also help partnerships to maintain a balanced focus on national priorities and local needs.

The JIT has a small core staff but draws on a pool of people, the 'Action Group', who are managers, clinicians, practitioners and others with direct experience of working in health and social care partnerships.

The JIT also identified a number of initial themes which it wished to pursue, with a view to sharing learning across partnerships. These included housing within health and social care partnerships; integrated transport across ambulance, local authority and community transport providers; intermediate care – a revised enthusiasm compared to earlier years (Petch, 2003); better use of resources, including the development of practical arrangements for joint commissioning, pooled budgets, and optimum use of property and equipment; managed clinical networks; and performance management and user/carer involvement. The list suggests the determination of the team to get to grips with some of the key components of the partnership agenda.

Initially established for two years, the JIT was still in operation at the time of writing (2007). Its website (www.jitscotland.org.uk) offers a range of resources, including a 'knowledge bank' and a number of publications. It also details the developments which have taken place within each theme and identifies a number of additional activities which are being pursued. For example, *Connecting Partnerships* (JIT, 2006) outlines a framework for supporting leadership, effective management and service innovations across health and social care partnerships through formal links between different partnerships receiving intensive support. These links would be facilitated by the JIT in the first instance but the hope is that the contact and shared learning will extend beyond this period of support.

Ladder of Support and Intervention

Following a consultation period during the first part of the year, Circular CCD12/2004 (*Community Care and Health (Scotland) Act 2002: Ministerial Powers of Intervention – Guidance on Ladder of Support and Intervention*) was issued in November 2004. As detailed in Chapter Three, Section 17 of the Community Care and Health (Scotland) Act 2002 had introduced powers that allow, where there are concerns over performance, intervention directing the partner agencies to implement joint working arrangements. The power is to be used as a last resort where improvement through other means appears unlikely; the emphasis is on the provision of support. A ladder of escalating support and intervention is outlined.

The circular acknowledged that there are few explicit targets for community care but suggested that concerns may be triggered by certain performance indicators:

- non-achievement of targets for delayed discharge;
- JPIAF measures;
- NHS Performance Assessment Framework (PAF)/Accountability Review;
- achievement of Local Improvement Targets;
- outcomes/targets for Community Health Partnerships;
- auditable criteria for Better Outcomes for Older People on good, integrated services (see below).

The approach is outlined at para. 31:

> Given that Ministerial intervention is a last resort, the evidence would have to demonstrate serious or sustained poor performance, which was unlikely to improve without intervention, even after support had been provided. The Act reinforces the point that 'improvement' includes better outcomes for people using services.

Where there are concerns, the first step on the ladder would be a meeting between the local partnership and Scottish Executive representatives to discuss the areas of concern. The local partnership would be expected within eight weeks to submit a Local Joint Working Improvement Plan. The partnership could set up an Internal Assessment Team or have access to the Joint

Improvement Team to assist in the preparation of the report, which would need to include actions, timescales, and the process for measuring outcomes. The Scottish Executive would in turn be required to respond to the improvement plan within four weeks; if the plan was not deemed satisfactory, the Joint Improvement Team would be asked to agree a Joint Working Action Plan with the partnership agencies. If the implementation of this action plan was not satisfactory, the local partners would then be consulted on the JIT's plan to intervene. Partnerships would be given a report on the continuing areas of concern and given four weeks within which to respond. If the response is deemed unsatisfactory, a direction will be issued to the local partnership. The actions that can be enforced are the delegation of functions and pooling of budgets under Section 15 of the 2002 Act; payments to one another under Sections 13 and 14; or other joint arrangements under Schedule 4 of the Regulations. Where necessary there is the possibility of fast tracking, moving directly to intervention.

Better Outcomes for Older People

In July 2004 the Scottish Executive issued for consultation a framework for joint services for older people titled *Better Outcomes for Older People.*

> The purpose of the Framework is to encourage the development and mainstreaming of joint services, which form one element of a wide range of joint working activities now in place across Scotland. (p. 4)

The title encapsulated the growing emphasis on an outcomes focus, a shift to ensuring the delivery of outcomes that are making a difference to individuals' lives (Petch, Miller and Cook, 2005). User outcomes have featured on research agendas for some years, most noticeably at the Social Policy Research Unit (Qureshi, 2001; Glendinning *et al.*, 2006), but over the last two years this emphasis has accelerated both north and south of the Border. The Department of Health (2006) White Paper *Our Health, Our Care, Our Say* specified seven core outcomes to be the focus for service delivery: improved health and well-being; making a positive contribution; economic well-being; freedom from discrimination; improved quality of life; choice and control; personal dignity. *Better Outcomes for Older People* acknowledges the increasing focus on outcomes north of the Border, including the adoption of the four national outcomes detailed above.

The consultation document recognised that to date there had been a greater focus on structure and process than on outcomes:

> The focus on the Joint Future Agenda needs now to be on achieving better outcomes for people and their carers. Joint structures and processes are well embedded and it is now necessary to use them to achieve better results. (p. 30)

Given the discussion of the evidence base for partnership working in Chapter Two, it is interesting to note the unqualified assertions that 'joint services can deliver better outcomes for individuals and their carers' (p. 17) and 'seamless services and a continuum of care are essential for improved outcomes' (p. 19); indeed that 'Implementation of Joint Future, e.g. joint management and joint resourcing of community care services, and single shared assessment ... are improving outcomes for older people' (p. 16). There is, however, an attempt to introduce systematic evaluation of the extent to which the specified outcomes are being achieved in the process of setting the Local Improvement Targets specified above. Action Four of the framework makes this explicit:

> When reviewing or designing services, local partnerships should develop joint services that deliver improved outcomes for individuals and their carers. These outcomes should have been agreed by the local partnerships with people who use services and their carers. These will assist in the achievement of Local Improvement Targets. (p. 7)

Better Outcomes for Older People can be seen as the Scottish equivalent of the *National Service Framework for Older People* in England (Department of Health, 2001a). It was developed by the Joint Services Group that had been established by the JFIAG to promote the implementation of joint services. What is perhaps most significant is the presumption for joint services, 'a platform for the development of joint services', with an implicit assumption that the case for their superiority has been established.

As part of the development of the framework, seven consultation events were held with older people across Scotland, including two involving black and minority ethnic groups. Five roadshows for representatives from local authorities and NHS boards and an event for community care providers were also held. The roadshows identified a number of key themes which underpin the framework and are listed below:

- involving as wide a range of stakeholders as possible when planning joint services, including providers from the private and voluntary sector, people who use services and carers;
- involving individuals and carers in care decisions so that care is person centred;
- information sharing is a key to effective service delivery (e.g. assessments should be shared appropriately with private and voluntary sector providers);
- more focus needs to be on preventative services such as rapid response teams and falls prevention, as opposed to the current NHSScotland focus on acute services;

- reducing the number of care staff who come into contact with an individual;

- housing providers are not yet an integral part of the Joint Future Agenda, and need to be engaged more fully (p. 78).

The framework was comprehensive. It set out the needs of an ageing population and argued for the supremacy of 'joint and integrated services'. Three principles were identified as key to the framework: person-centred care, an outcome focus, and whole system working for health, housing and social care services. The key messages from the framework are listed below.

- Joint services can deliver better outcomes for individuals and their carers.

- Individuals and their carers must be involved more effectively, and local partners should act on what they say.

- Local partnerships must use a whole system approach when commissioning joint services. There should be a step change in improving and extending joint commissioning.

- Providing joint services should involve health, housing and social care providers, whether statutory organisations, the independent sector or carers. This approach is essential if sustainable solutions to the more complex problems facing local partnerships, e.g. the growth in the older population and delayed discharges, are to be achieved.

- Joint services can meet the growing need for specialist services such as those for people with dementia, sensory impairment or mental health needs.

- Resources should be brought together, devolved, and made accessible to practitioners at the point of delivery and across agency boundaries.

- The changes in this Framework, such as the move from piloting to mainstreaming joint services, do not necessarily require more resources. Service redesign can assist the funding of better joint services, by reducing duplication or by more effective use of scarce resources.

- The benefits of more integrated working and joint services will be achieved if staff and managers are engaged in the change process, are enthusiastic about it, and can see how they personally can deliver better outcomes for older people. This may require staff and managers to focus more on the needs of individuals and their carers rather than on their professional roles and organisational structures.

- Joint performance management, both nationally and locally, is essential so that local partnerships can demonstrate better outcomes for individuals. (p. 17)

Better Outcomes for Older People sought to clarify their definition of joint services whilst recognising that a single definition is not possible or desirable – 'the value of joint services is their flexibility, their responsiveness to local needs, and their ability to deliver better outcomes for individuals' (p. 13). This document is significant for explicitly stating the somewhat different direction from England:

> Organisational or structural change is not a pre-requisite for improving outcomes for individuals and their carers. Scotland has not widely endorsed the view (commonly held in England) that care trusts or similar new joint organisational structures are essential for better outcomes. More integrated working, which includes joint management arrangements and joint resourcing, is the preferred option, together with clear strategic arrangements, performance management and evaluation of outcomes. Seamless services and a continuum of care are essential for improved outcomes. (p. 19)

The Joint Services Group suggested there were three types of joint service; each model could operate in either a generic or a specialist context. The first of the three types they isolated was the integrated team. The function of the team may be assessment only; assessment, care management and service provision; or service provision. Community learning disability teams and community mental health teams are common examples of specialist teams, while rapid response teams and community rehabilitation teams often have a more generic remit. The second model refers to jointly organised or commissioned services that are jointly provided by local partners, for example a multi-agency assessment and screening service for older people. The service usually extends beyond a single team and there may be a single manager and a single budget. The third arrangement is services that are jointly commissioned but delivered by one organisation, for example augmented home care services. There may be arrangements for direct access to these services by both health and local authority staff.

The Joint Services Group also suggested that joint services could be considered as a continuum, 'progressing along a spectrum of complexity and effectiveness'. Level one signifies jointly planned services; level two services are jointly commissioned; level three services are jointly delivered; while level four indicates that services are integrated. The key developments in the progression through the levels is identified in checklist form.

Better Outcomes for Older People was very much a document to assist detailed implementation. It offered a range of checklists for the practical achievement of joint working and defined a total of 22 actions to be taken under the framework. For the majority of actions a milestone was identified for achievement by December 2005; an overarching action was that all local partnerships were to review the potential for joint services on an ongoing basis. Shared aims and objectives, agreed outcomes and current and future resources for service provision were to be identified. The specific actions can be grouped according to their focus.

Principles underpinning joint service design – services were to be based on a person-centred approach, were to focus on delivering improved outcomes as defined by older people and their unpaid carers, and were to use a whole system approach as explored by the Audit Commission (2002). Information was to be provided for the public on available services.

Commissioning and implementing joint services – partnerships were encouraged to actively develop their joint commissioning processes, agreeing the joint services likely to improve outcomes. Services were to be commissioned in line with the national policy for a shift in the balance of care towards maintaining people in their own homes, with careful attention to effective involvement of the voluntary and private sectors, to mainstreaming pilot projects, and to the development of the infrastructure necessary for commissioning. Effective change management was to be put in place as necessary, for example human resource strategies and governance frameworks for joint services.

An active and healthy life in older age – the role of joint services in health promotion was identified, including income maximisation and advocacy. Local partners were to review and develop their strategic framework and joint services for health promotion, preventative and early intervention services for older people as part of their local planning agreements.

Promoting independence at home for older people – partnerships were to develop more care at home, equipment and adaptations, and day care services; they were to review their involvement with housing providers and to develop more joint services such as extra care housing; and they were to ensure that when services were developed under Supporting People this was done in a way that promoted integration.

Joint services for enhanced care – enhanced care services were to be developed by partnerships to ensure that as people's needs increase there are services to avoid inappropriate admission to care home or hospital and to provide support following a hospital stay. Key elements in enhanced care are rapid response and early discharge, rehabilitation, step-up and step-down services providing short stays in alternative accommodation, and palliative and terminal care.

Joint services for carers of older people – partnerships were asked to engage more fully with carers in developing and reviewing strategies or action plans and to provide more joint services for carers; they were also encouraged to make more joint use of available funding streams to provide longer-term services.

Joint services for older people with additional needs – partnerships were to review the potential for joint services for older people with additional needs such as learning or physical disabilities, were to incorporate joint arrangements into mental health service developments, and were to refer to the needs of older people with drug and alcohol problems.

Joint services for older people with dementia and their carers – joint services were to be included as part of the development or review by local partnerships of their joint strategic framework for dementia services.

Evaluating joint services together – performance management and evaluation was to be a core element of joint service developments, with outcomes for individuals and carers built in from the start and systematic arrangements for collecting the views of people who use services. Nine auditable criteria relating to the joint aspects of services were identified. These range from the outcomes and objectives of the joint service, the involvement of people who use services and their carers, and delegated authority for decision making and allocation of resources, to effective record keeping and awareness of good practice, new legislation and current research.

Following a twelve-week consultation period, the Framework for Joint Services for Older People was formally issued in May 2005 under Circular 1/2005. There was some re-ordering in the report and streamlining of the actions but the general tenor of the report had been well received. Three key actions were highlighted at this stage. Partnerships were asked to undertake an initial review of their existing joint services and the potential for development and to report by December 2005 under the JPIAF for 2005/06. They were asked to keep services under continuous review and to report on the development and expansion of services in the JPIAF for 2006/07. Finally, evaluation of the framework including outcomes for older people was to be reported in JPIAF 11 of the Local Improvement Targets in 2004/05 and 2005/06.

National Outcomes Framework

In January 2006 the Joint Future Unit circulated a letter to partnerships, 'Joint Future: The Outcomes Approach – Next Steps'. An earlier letter in August

2005 had expressed concern at the lack of apparent progress reflected in the draft JPIAF submissions for 2004/05. Partnerships had been invited to submit further evidence and following this the overall assessment had been more positive. One third of the 32 partnerships were rated as demonstrating 'good progress' and nearly half 'steady progress'. For those receiving the judgement 'improvement required', the Joint Future Unit remains in contact. The Unit had also sought feedback from partnerships on barriers in the JPIAF reporting process. Issues highlighted included IT and the need to develop robust local performance cultures; reporting timeframes; and the need for more structured support for partnerships on the process.

This letter also highlighted the importance attached to developing the outcomes approach across all client groups during the year 2006/07. The Ministerial Steering Group expected local partners to:

- embed the outcomes approach in a comprehensive joint performance framework;
- shift from 'in-house' reporting of performance within partnerships and to the Executive, to regular public reporting;
- progress targets from being 'annual' to medium/long term, whilst ensuring that they remain challenging.

CCD5/2005 summarised the JPIAF requirement for 2005/06. With the increasing emphasis on outcomes rather than process, JPIAF 4 on joint resourcing was being dropped. Otherwise the indicators remained as in 2004/05: JPIAF 10 – whole system indicator; JPIAF 11 – Local Improvement Targets (LITs); JPIAF 6 – SSA; and JPIAF 8 – access to resources following SSA across agency boundaries. Partnerships were to prepare for reporting on local targets for all community care groups; the first full LIT response would be required for the period 2007/08, with preparatory work throughout 2006/07 on extending JPIAF 10 and JPIAF 11 across all user groups. There was also a belated recognition of the housing contribution, with housing and accommodation issues expected to feature as key elements.

The most recent circular, CCD2/2007, signals a marked shift in the development process. In it, the Joint Future Implementation Group is now looking for more radical progress towards an outcome focus:

> While Local Improvement Targets have been the key driver of progress towards the outcomes focus in Community Care, the national partnership is concerned at the level of progress and the lack of consistency on performance between partnerships. (para. 3)

The Group has therefore established a National Outcomes Project chaired by the Chief Executive of NHS Lanarkshire and charged with taking the outcome approach to 'a new level'. The specific objectives for the project are defined as:

- achieving consistency of understanding of the outcomes agenda;
- developing a suite of national outcomes, performance measures and targets to drive joint performance in community care;
- identifying the information needed to performance manage this agenda both locally and nationally;
- reducing the burden of scrutiny in community care, as much as possible;
- developing proposals for a coherent performance management system.

An external agency was commissioned to work with the NHS on the fast track development of a performance framework for all community care groups. It was anticipated that this would comprise four national outcomes, 20 high level national performance measures and a number of national targets. As a result of this initiative, JPIAF reporting requirements for 2006/07 were modified, the anticipated LITs across all user groups for 2007/08 no longer being required during what was portrayed as a period of transition. 'The extent to which JPIAF continues under the new outcomes agenda from 2007/08 onwards will be determined in the coming months' (Circular CCD2/2007, para. 24).

The Joint Improvement Team had already commissioned work to integrate user and carer experiences of health and social care partnership working into performance management measures. Specifically this was working to develop a toolkit to support health and social care partnerships to:

- capture information on the outcomes they are delivering to service users and carers; and
- use that data on user and carer experiences to inform performance management, service improvement and the reviewing of individual packages of support.

This work builds on a research project funded by the Department of Health under its Modernising Adult Social Care research initiative and conducted at the University of Glasgow (Petch *et al.*, 2007). The project had explored the extent to which health and social care partnerships (three in Scotland, twelve in England) were delivering the outcomes valued by service users. It used a framework of outcomes based on those developed by the Social Policy Research Unit and referenced above but modified in the light of further review. The framework is summarised in Table 5.1.

The JIT work is proceeding in three phases. Reports on the first two phases are available from the JIT website. The first phase involved two workshops exploring the extent to which partnerships were currently working with user perspectives. Although a range of strategies were cited, it emerged that very few partnerships had engaged users and carers in setting Local Improvement Targets. During the second phase detailed work took place with three partner-

Table 5.1 User-defined outcomes

Quality of Life	Process	Change
• safety	• being listened to	• improving mobility
• having things to do	• being valued and	• restoring skills and
• social contact	treated with respect	confidence
• staying as well as	• choice	• reducing symptoms
you can	• responsiveness	
• living where you	• reliability	
want		
• living life as you		
want		
• dealing with stigma/		
discrimination		

ships – Fife, Orkney and East Lothian. This explored the use and development of the original User Defined Service Evaluation Tool (UDSET) in two distinct ways: service evaluation and review of individual outcomes. For the latter the tool was developed as an Outcomes Based Review Form and in Orkney provided the basis for discussion with individuals at annual review. A Carer Defined Service Evaluation Tool (CDSET) and Outcomes Based Carer Review Form are also being developed, and their use will be explored as part of the third phase. The potential for quantifying data gathered from individual reviews will also be explored.

Meanwhile the National Outcomes Board has progressed the development of the National Outcomes Framework for Community Care. The overall objectives for the framework are to:

- focus on benefits for service users and carers;
- drive performance in community care;
- re-focus on partnership working;
- ensure joint responsibility for service delivery; and
- clarify reporting both locally and nationally.

Following consultation at national events, a letter was circulated from the Joint Future Unit on 4 April 2007. This reiterated the need for cultural change:

> Joint Future has been the catalyst for cultural shift in which joint working is now the norm. But we still need to find better ways of delivering services – quality services that are focused, personalised, joined up and accountable to the service user. The outcomes framework provides the basis for that approach and will, we believe, make a real difference to joint performance in community care.

The draft set of national outcome measures was specified. These comprise four high level outcomes – improved health; improved well-being; improved social inclusion; and improved independence and responsibility – and 16 performance measures. A follow-up letter on 17 April 2007 provided further details on each of the draft measures. They focus on users' satisfaction with services; waiting times; quality of assessment; shifting the balance of care; carers' well-being; unscheduled care; and the identification of 'people at risk'. The Board has appointed a Design Authority to oversee the development of the measures. At the initial stage of development, it would appear that despite best efforts, several of the measures are still some distance removed from direct outcomes, with several still labelled as 'proxy'.

The role of Local Improvement Targets has now been clarified. Partnerships will still be expected to develop these but they will be used at the local level in the context of the national framework. The Joint Future Unit letter of 4 April states: 'Each partnership should set their own, having regard to the national outcomes, national performance measures and emerging national targets, but also reflecting local circumstances and priorities' (para. 18). This reflects the switch in emphasis from centralised performance monitoring to greater responsibility and autonomy at the local level. The aim, as expressed in the 'implementation letter' of 4 April is to 'support partnerships' flexibility to deliver locally'. For the first year from April 2007, partnerships will be expected to report on the four national outcomes and six of the sixteen performance measures. The first in a bulletin series for the National Outcomes Framework was issued in June 2007. Tantalisingly, this volume has to conclude its presentation on the evolution of the Joint Future Agenda activity at this point on the timeline.

CHAPTER 6

Brave New World
or Emperor's New Clothes?

I think it's a nice thing, you feel as if you're in a little net and
they're all working together to make sure that you are fine.

The Joint Future Agenda is an evolving process. Key shifts in emphasis have already been identified in Chapter Five. The degree of central direction has been more recently relaxed to place more emphasis on local determination of performance targets. At the same time the National Outcomes Project has given a clear indication that an outcomes focus is mandatory. This final chapter will reflect on the development to mid 2007 and offer general commentary within the context of partnership working. It should be noted that, perhaps surprisingly, there has been no systematic evaluation of the impact of the Joint Future initiatives, whether at service level in terms of models of working or inter-professional relationships, or at the individual level in terms of user and carer outcomes. Any appraisal therefore has to rely on a more disparate mix of modest empirical evidence, operational wisdom, and observed practice.

Interim snapshots

The Nuffield Centre for Community Care Studies conducted two reviews of progress with the implementation of community care policy in Scotland. The first Nuffield Barometer reported in 2002 and the second in 2004. At both stages a telephone interview was conducted with a key respondent in each of the 32 local authorities. A core set of questions was repeated at each survey, with additional questions in Barometer One on older people and in Barometer Two on support for adults aged 16 to 65. The focus was broader than the Joint Future Agenda, but increasingly the requirements for partnership working can be seen as impacting across service provision. Although now somewhat historical, it is of interest to highlight a number of the headlines from Barometer Two. These reflect progress a decade after the implementation of the key community care provisions of the 1990 NHS and Community Care Act and two years into the Joint Future Agenda; they also highlight a number of issues of enduring relevance.

By the time of the second interviews in autumn 2003, all 32 local authorities had a single shared assessment process in place, compared with 25 in 2001. The majority considered that SSA was now synonymous with a community care assessment. The Joint Future Group report had led to authorities adopting Carenap (sometimes adapted) or their own tool based on the core data set. Twenty-eight authorities reported that their assessment tool covered all client groups, with a further four authorities having a tool for older people only. Six authorities identified the SSA tool as the basis for their carers assessment tool. The proportion of the assessments conducted by health professionals was low, however, with the highest level reported being 25 per cent. Responses suggested that training was leading to an increase in health-led assessments, with early supported discharge from hospital acting as a driver.

Respondents raised two issues in relation to SSA which recur throughout discussion of partnership working. The first of these is the protocol for sharing confidential information relating to individuals between agencies. This can often be cited as a barrier to progressing partnership working without consulting with individual users and carers who may be only too happy for such information to be shared; indeed they may assume that the information provided to one professional is shared with others. The second enduring issue is the availability of IT systems that are both accessible and shared. At Barometer Two, just over half of authorities were piloting IT systems with health while in the remaining partnerships it was under discussion. With housing they were more likely to be under discussion than piloted.

A number of initiatives within the Joint Future arena were amongst the 36 projects funded under the Modernising Government Fund in December 2000. They sought to tackle the problem 'that the information available to support the delivery of effective, citizen-focused social care services in Scotland is of variable quality and not comparable from one agency or authority to the next' (Scottish Executive, 2003c, p. 10). This e-Care programme focused on common infrastructure, on data standards and data sharing protocols, and also on improved information sharing between practitioners and service users. Indeed the report on the fund (Scottish Executive, 2003c) quotes an interview response which well illustrates the user preference for information to be shared – 'so that's why the district nurse always seems to turn up just when the home help is taking me to the day care centre for my carpet bowls' (p. 10). Specific projects focused on:

- SSA services to older people and adults with mental health problems (Lanarkshire, Argyll and Clyde);
- a joint equipment store including a mobile service and internet access to stock control (Borders); and
- SSA occupational therapy services (Forth Valley).

These were located within the overarching framework of the National Joint Future ICT Strategy, *My Information: My Key to a Joint Future*. This sought to enable partner agencies, under the Local Partnership Agreements, to establish shared ICT support for key operational processes, and to provide a supportive framework for the cultural change from 'owning' service user information to acting as 'custodians'. Developments included the creation of an e-Care store, safeguarding shared information by storing it separately from either network; a method for cross referencing NHS and social work patient/user identifiers; and a template for information-sharing protocols, with templates and linked documentation.

A further nine e-Care projects were funded under the second round of the Modernising Government Fund. These sought to promote a common language and to create standard user-focused data definitions and data sets to support information sharing in order to progress effective joint service provision.

Barometer Two also highlighted a key feature of the Joint Future implementation. Certainly in the initial years housing has returned to the role of the invisible partner, the partnership agenda having predominantly focused on health and social care. Only in the most recent pronouncements has there been acknowledgment of the need to embrace the housing contribution. The creation of a number of departments combining social work and housing had raised the profile, while Supporting People was reported to have introduced a new opportunity for social work and housing to jointly assess service users for housing support and to access each other's IT systems.

A very practical manifestation of partnership working is whether partners operate a joint equipment store. Twenty-five agencies reported a joint equipment store at Barometer Two, an increase of ten from the previous survey; nine authorities indicated they were also working with other local authorities in the operation of their store. In general there was an IT system to access the store, together with a database for tracking the equipment. Authorities cited some problems with joint funding as a result of health not processing their bills or operating on deficit funding which meant they were unable to invest any money into the store. Opportunities had been taken in some authorities to use delayed discharge funding to augment the store.

A particularly interesting feature of the Barometer surveys was the extent of joint work with the Local Health Care Co-operatives (LHCCs), in particular local authority staff attending the LHCC meetings. This was increasingly evident: most commonly the person attending was the Head of Community Care or the Area Social Work Manager. Areas of joint working between local authorities and LHCCs were extensive, indicating a varied approach within each locality. Most frequently cited were prevention of admission / delayed discharge, Joint Future, and mental health. Joint Future and mental health were the most common priorities also, together with Community Health Partnerships (CHPs). At this stage some authorities felt that the CHP agenda was pushing the community care agenda into the background or that the focus was too centred on the clinical/medical agenda:

> There is tension with LHCCs, as social work is far down the priority list while Health have their eye on Community Health Partnerships. There is tension between this and Joint Future. They (Community Health Partnerships and Joint Future) are distracting each other. (unpublished interview)

This reflects a common observation at the time that different sections within the Scottish Executive were operating within a silo mentality. Another area of some confusion was the continuation of community care plans. Nineteen authorities indicated that locality plans were in place for LHCCs. Others felt that the joint community care plan was used by the LHCC as their plan, while five respondents considered that the joint plan was becoming redundant because of the planning around LHCCs, Joint Future and Local Partnership Agreements:

> Somebody needs to address what we should do with joint community care plans. Other plans do not reflect this now. We did not do a joint community care plan last year.

> There has not been a formal joint community care plan for four years. We suspect we will end up with for example older people's strategy, mental health strategy etc. (unpublished interviews)

There is an irony if a system designed to promote collaboration may in turn lead to fragmentation.

All authorities reported having joint posts, most frequently joint learning disability posts (10), Joint Future implementation manager posts (10) and integrated mental health posts (8). There were a variety of arrangements, for example single managers for joint services, sometimes employed by social work and sometimes by the NHS. A number of respondents said that they were taking the integration at a slow pace and that integrated posts had to be carefully planned: 'single management has to have a purpose; it is not a purpose in its own right'. The three most frequently mentioned achievements in joint working were the development of SSA, integrated/co-located teams, and delayed discharge / rapid response teams. These were four times more likely to be mentioned than other achievements.

Respondents were asked whether their agency used generic workers, defined as workers who undertook both health and social care tasks. Eighteen authorities indicated they had workers of this type; in ten of the authorities they operated from a specialist team. The host agency was the local authority in thirteen of the cases, health in two, and joint in three. The majority of authorities did not charge as the service was for four weeks or less or was personal care and therefore free. A small number of authorities used their existing home care charging policy to determine charges. Increased integration between social work and health offered opportunities for joint training and for aligning staff. In Barometer One, the most frequent area for joint training had been moving and handling; this was now replaced by SSA.

As detailed in Chapter Four under 'Local Partnership Agreements', the Joint Future Agenda is accompanied by a range of human resource challenges. Fifteen councils at this date had no plans or were unaware of any plans to bring terms and conditions into alignment. Fourteen councils did have plans, either progressed through a Joint Future Partnership Group or a Joint Staff Forum. One council reiterated the challenges:

> This is a nightmare. There is a Joint Partnership Forum involving two personnel departments. It needs a strategic approach using different job evaluations. In an evaluation of one joint manager post the local authority evaluated it as around £30,000 per annum. Health evaluated the same post at around £20,000 because it was not a nurse.

The potential models for aligning or pooling financial resources were outlined in Chapter Five. Local authority respondents were reluctant to talk about their financial frameworks for community care and health under the term 'pooled budgets'. Only one council indicated they had a 'tiny' pooled budget. The majority considered that their financial framework approximated to aligned budgets. This accords with the retreat from the aspiration for pooled budgets. Seven authorities had signed or were in the process of signing a partnership agreement and nine already had an accountant or joint finance or Joint Future group overseeing the development of aligned budgets. One council stated:

> The council is operating aligned budgets in joint resourcing. The pot is detailed in the Local Partnership Agreement. There is a governance and accountability framework supporting liabilities and mediation of disputes. The joint finance group oversees the framework to support implementation. We are also processing an internal audit plan and corporate risk profile.

As demonstrated in the matrix for integrated working in Chapter Three, policy directives can be an important driver. This can be illustrated from the Barometer in respect of rapid response teams, a requirement from *Community Care: A Joint Future*. Seventeen authorities reported having a rapid response team, six had a combine rapid response / early discharge team, and nine used a different term but provided the same function. The large majority of these teams had been established in the immediate wake of the Joint Future report.

Embryonic evidence

The absence of any large-scale evaluation of the impact of the Joint Future initiative has already been noted. Evidence on the impact of the implementation of the Joint Future Agenda is therefore fragmentary. Bruce and Forbes (2005a, 2005b) have reported on some early scrutiny of the Local Partnership Agreements (LPAs). Based on interviews in 2003 with key respondents from agencies covering four LPA areas, five areas presenting challenges to the Joint Future Agenda were identified. The balance between central and local control, an enduring debate on the Scottish policy scene, was considered by many local respondents to have tipped too far towards central management. There had been an attempt to impose a 'one size fits all' solution, with the imposition of unrealistic timescales and targets and a drive for quick political wins. Respondents reflected that there had been an oppressive interference in local planning, giving little time for local ownership of the agenda or pursuit of the best local solutions. One suspects that this sentiment would have been even stronger if these interviews had been conducted in the wake of the subsequent raft of JPIAF indicators.

The four other areas highlighted by this study were organisational, cultural, financial and political differences. Organisational boundaries, for example, led to difficulties in developing generic or hybrid workers; management styles differed; and individuals from one agency knew little of the operation of the other. The failure of agencies to proceed with pooled budgets meant that many of the financial wrangles still continued, while the differing accountability structures of health and local authorities led to some local authority suspicion of initiatives which could be construed as centralist. The authors conclude:

> Joint working is something of a quantum leap and while there is clear understanding within the Scottish Executive about the need for joint working in the delivery of community care, evidence about how exactly this is to be achieved is less abundant. (2005b, p. 336)

The depressing indictment of this statement is that, as demonstrated in Chapter One, there is significant evidence at least on the process of partnership working which could have predicted much of the scenario outlined by these respondents. To what extent could implementation have been more effective if this evidence base had been woven into the implementation process?

Reference can be made to another (unpublished) study conducted by the author and designed to explore the development of partnership working in one health board area in Scotland. This area had developed an early pilot initiative in integrated working, and subsequent interviews with health and social care professionals were designed to assess the extent to which partnership working had become mainstream. The timing of the study (2003–04), however, revealed a preoccupation amongst respondents with a single aspect of the Joint Future Agenda, the detail of delivering single shared assessment. Significantly, not all respondents, particularly from health, had appreciated that this was a non-negotiable initiative from the Scottish Executive rather than a locally led programme. It is easy for those centrally involved in policy development to forget the layers of communication and information that have to be negotiated to reach front-line practitioners.

A range of familiar barriers was raised. There were professional differences in approach to the assessment process, and indeed duplication of assessments where referral systems were not yet synchronised. Attitudes towards autonomy and risk varied, and there were different levels of authority in terms of access to resources. Individuals did not always feel equipped to complete all aspects of the SSA; health professionals leading an assessment could be wary of becoming involved in the financial aspects of assessment, arguing that this was not their expertise. IT systems were often incompatible and debates continued around interpretations of confidentiality. Respondents often complained about lack of administrative support and their struggles to complete ill-designed forms. Ongoing responsibility, for care management and review, was not always clear. There was evidence of the development of informal strategies to navigate the assessment process, for example health professionals diverting individuals requesting an assessment to social work in order to avoid being the first point of contact (and therefore the assessor). Nonetheless, many respondents were in favour of moving towards co-location of health and social care staff; it was deemed important, however, to ensure clarity of roles and of purpose.

The findings of this study epitomise a recurring issue in evaluation of partnership working. To what extent are difficulties encountered an inevitable feature of the evolution process, or to what extent do they signify more fundamental challenges? Too often evaluations are conducted at the stage where they identify inevitable teething problems rather than more substantive barriers. Scrutiny of individual initiatives such as SSA brings with it, however, the danger of becoming fixated on process at the expense of longer-term outcomes. It can be difficult to interpret these fragmented snapshots in the absence of a longer-term evaluation of the Joint Future initiative.

Further evidence on the more general perspectives of professionals towards the partnership working agenda in respect of older people is offered by Hubbard and Themessl-Huber (2005). Managers and front-line staff from health and social care in six health board areas were interviewed. Analysis of the 34 interviews grouped findings into six key areas. The need for a *fundamental change in thinking* was acknowledged, with time to allow this to happen rather than undue pressure. The importance of working with *professional roles* was highlighted: in working together individuals wanted to retain their professional identities but be open to taking on new roles. Familiar patterns of working, for example referral routes, could be difficult to overcome, and access to services could be constrained by agency barriers. Many respondents acknowledged the importance of developing *whole systems working* but were very much aware of the challenges in knitting together the different elements to deliver a strategic vision. Despite the apparent central direction of the Joint Future Agenda, a range of approaches to *initiating joint working* was discerned. *Exchanging knowledge about patients and services* was considered key to partnership working, but different areas adopted different approaches. The potential of *information technology*, and the barrier of its absence, was cited by many. Finally, *geographical size and coterminosity* were considered by some respondents to be factors influencing the extent of partnership working. Hubbard and Themessl-Huber highlight again the paucity of evidence on the impact of these factors on the service user. 'A whole systems perspective that utilises and synthesises knowledge of patients and professionals is needed so that new knowledge conducive to joint working can spark and ignite' (p. 384).

The art of partnership working

A set of five laws for integrating health and social care was formulated by Leutz (1999) and revisited six years later (Leutz, 2005). These offer a final basis for reflecting on progress with the Joint Future Agenda. As originally presented the five laws stated:

- You can integrate some of the services for all the people, all the services for some of the people, but you can't integrate all the services for all people.
- Integration costs before it pays.
- Your integration is my fragmentation.
- You can't integrate a square peg and a round hole.
- The one who integrates calls the tune.

The return to the laws in 2005 acknowledged the value of certain features of partnership working: the single access point and the 'one-stop' service; and the promotion of different levels of collaborative working – linkage, co-ordination and full integration. Some new guidelines were formulated: 'help not hassle for physicians'; 'put the right person/organisation in charge of integration'; 'support integration financially'; 'all integration is local'; 'keep it simple'; 'don't try to integrate everything'; 'integration isn't built in a day'. What is being suggested is a greater flexibility in tailoring a particular partnership response to the specifics of the individual situation.

Perhaps it is the original first and fourth laws which should head the reflection. History has dictated the current distinct and separate structures for health and social care delivery. The current debates on collaboration, partnership, integration result from this historical legacy; a different, unified structure would pre-empt at least some of the strategies detailed above. The cross-agency provision of the Community Care and Health (Scotland) Act 2002 (and the 1999 Health Act flexibilities) would be unnecessary, and at least some of the tribal divisions and silos would be eliminated. What is difficult to predict is the extent to which co-location of interests is both a necessary and a sufficient solution.

The situation in Northern Ireland has already been referenced in Chapter One, suggesting that co-location may not in itself guarantee integrated activity. Moreover there is no assurance against internal divisions within unified structures. Contemporary developments in England suggest there may have been some stalling of the partnership working agenda. There have been a number of high profile fall-outs between agencies at the forefront of partnership working – Wiltshire, Brent; while the significance of the Care Trust initiative has been in the handful of developments that have proceeded. Leutz's fourth law was based in part on the conflicts inherent in acute and long-term care, in systems distinguished by very different funding systems. The return to cost shunting evidenced in the recent fall-outs and the inability to achieve pooled budgets suggests a validity to this law.

One of the first significant activities following the establishment of the Scottish Parliament was the Inquiry into the Delivery of Community Care conducted by the Health and Community Care Committee (Scottish Parliament, 2000). An interesting shift occurred during the course of the Inquiry, from an enthusiasm and presumption for a unified structure to an acknowledgement that the upheaval of structural change could be counterproductive and that a lead agency model could be preferable:

> The Committee does not believe that a single body with a single budget will in itself solve the problems associated with the current arrangements. In taking evidence from community care managers and professionals from Northern Ireland, the Committee was struck by the extent to which multi-professional working can still be elusive even when it is the case there that a unitary body is responsible for primary care and social services. (para. 70)

In the event the publication of the Inquiry report was rapidly followed by that from the Joint Future Group. In their responses to both, the Scottish Executive set in train the evolving Joint Future Agenda which has been explored in this volume. Reports on the JPIAF returns offer a perspective, albeit a partial and central one, on the extent to which progress has been achieved.

Only most recently, however, has there been the shift to a recognition that the process of partnership working is far less important than the outcomes, and most specifically for the current context, the outcomes for service users and carers. Has the energy that has been committed to the implementation of Joint Future mechanisms resulted in different and improved outcomes for those on the receiving end of the arrangements? As highlighted in the earlier discussion of the evidence base for partnership working, the impact of partnership working on user outcomes is rarely addressed. Some tentative results in respect of specific health and social care partnership initiatives can be drawn from the project highlighted earlier (Petch *et al.*, 2007), but these are by no means definitive.

The most recent development in the Joint Future Agenda, the creation of a National Outcomes Framework, suggests that the journey may, somewhat belatedly, have reached this milestone. The extent to which the appropriate framework can be structured and, most importantly, whether this then demonstrates the effectiveness of the various components of the Joint Future initiative must be the focus of the next stage. At the same time the extent to which Community Health Partnerships become a key driver in the delivery of the Joint Future Agenda will be under close scrutiny.

Conclusion

A recent discussion by Hudson (2007) has drawn some interesting contrasts between the trajectories of partnership working north and south of the Border. He posits three potential dichotomies: coherence rather than choice; relationships rather than structures; and whole systems rather than ad hoc partnering. He suggests that in opting for an approach based more on coherence and whole systems, Scotland may be pursuing a course more compatible with partnership working than that emerging in England. In England, he contends, there are other competing discourses and policy imperatives such as market incentives which are likely to compete.

This exploration of partnership working as exemplified by the Joint Future Agenda in Scotland has highlighted a number of enduring tensions. These include:

- the balance between central and local control;
- the transition from a focus on the process of partnership working to consideration of the outcomes for individuals;
- the separation of early muddle from longer-term difficulties;
- the power of individual leadership versus organisational commitment;
- the promotion of individual professional identities against the need to develop new ways of working;
- the role of legislation and of sanctions in progressing an agenda.

It is important to acknowledge that on longer-term timescales progress on the partnership agenda does seem to be inching forward. There have, however, been a number of cul-de-sacs and dead-ends along the route. Pooled budgets were considered a step too far; there has been a retreat from a raft of performance indicators to the current wrestle with identifying outcomes which can determine whether partnership working is delivering for service users.

Key dimensions identified three years ago by the Joint Improvement Team as the 'way forward for partnerships' remain equally valid today: service redesign to achieve a whole systems approach; meaningful involvement of users and carers; closer partnerships with the independent sector; making the Joint Future Agenda a reality.

There is, at the time of writing, another nagging question. To what extent is partnership working still key to the policy agenda? There is a new focus on personalisation, on the individual service user becoming the key driver in determining the network of support which they access. The logic of such an approach would suggest that the agencies that will thrive are those that are favoured by service users and their support brokers because they are responsive to their needs. Perhaps the destiny of partnership working, the waxing and waning of different models, is destined to provide a constant organisational backcloth while front stage more immediate initiatives are brought to the fore.

References

Asthana, S., Richardson, S. and Halliday. J. (2002) 'Partnership working in public policy provision: a framework for evaluation', *Social Policy and Administration*, Vol. 36, No. 7, pp. 780–95

Audit Commission (1986) *Making a Reality of Community Care*, London: HMSO

Audit Commission (1998) *A Fruitful Partnership: Effective Partnership Working*, London: Audit Commission

Audit Commission (2000) *The Way to Go Home: Rehabilitation and Remedial Services for Older People*, London: The Stationery Office

Audit Commission (2002) *Integrated Services for Older People: Building a Whole System Approach in England*, London: Audit Commission

Banks, P. (2002) *Partnerships under Pressure: A Commentary on Progress in Partnership Working between the NHS and Local Government*, London: King's Fund

Barnes, M., Matka, E. and Sullivan, H. (2003) 'Evidence, understanding and complexity: evaluation in non-linear systems', *Evaluation*, Vol. 9, No. 3, pp. 262–82

Barnes, M., Bauld, L., Benzeval, M., Mackenzie, M., Sullivan, H. and Judge, K. (2005) *Health Action Zones: Partnerships for Health Equity*, London: Routledge

Beresford, P. and Trevillion, S. (1995) *Developing Skills for Community Care: A Collaborative Approach*, Aldershot: Arena

Brown, L., Tucker, C. and Domokos, T. (2002) *What Impact Does an Integrated Delivery of Health and Social Care Services Have on Older People Living in the Community, Compared with a Traditional Non-Integrated Approach?* Wiltshire County Council/University of Bath

Brown, L., Tucker, C. and Domokos, T. (2003) 'Evaluating the impact of integrated health and social care teams on older people living in the community', *Health and Social Care in the Community*, Vol. 11, No. 2, pp. 85–94

Bruce, A. and Forbes, T. (2005a) 'Delivering community care in Scotland: can local partnerships bridge the gap?', *Scottish Affairs*, Autumn

Bruce, A. and Forbes, T. (2005b) 'Joining up community care in Scotland', *British Journal of Health Care Management*, Vol. 11, No. 11, pp. 334–8

Cameron, A., Lart, R., Harrison, L., Macdonald, G. and Smith, R. (2000) *Factors Promoting and Obstacles Hindering Joint Working: A Systematic Review*, University of Bristol: School for Policy Studies

Care Development Group (2001) *Fair Care for Older People*, Edinburgh: Scottish Executive

Carter, D. and Woods, K. (eds) (2003) *Scotland's Health and Health Services*, London: Nuffield Trust

Clarke, J. and Glendinning, C. (2002) 'Partnership and the remaking of welfare governance', in Glendinning, C., Powell, M. and Rummery, K. (eds) (2002) *Partnerships, New Labour and the Governance of Welfare*, Bristol: The Policy Press

Commission for Healthcare Audit and Inspection (2006) *Living Well in Later Life*, London: Commission for Healthcare Audit and Inspection

Community Care Providers Scotland (2002) *A 'Joint Future' for Community Care: A Voluntary Sector Perspective*, Edinburgh: CCPS

Dalley, G. (1989) 'Professional ideology or organisational tribalism? The health service-social work divide', in Taylor, R. and Ford, J. (eds) (1989) *Social Work and Health Care*, London: Jessica Kingsley

Department of Health (1995*) Joint Commissioning for Project Leaders*, London: HMSO

Department of Health (1997a) *Developing Partnerships in Mental Health*, London, HMSO

Department of Health (1997b) *The New NHS: Modern, Dependable*, London: HMSO

Department of Health (1998a) *Modernising Social Services: Promoting Independence, Improving Protection, Raising Standards*, London: The Stationery Office

Department of Health (1998b) *Modernising Health and Social Services: National Priorities Guidance*, London: Department of Health

Department of Health (1998c) *Partnership in Action (New Opportunities for Joint Working between Health and Social Services): A Discussion Document*, London: Department of Health

Department of Health (1998d) *Modernising Mental Health Services: Safe, Sound and Supportive*, London: Department of Health

Department of Health (1999a) *A National Service Framework for Mental Health*, London: Department of Health

Department of Health (1999b) *Government Response to the First Report of the Health Committee on the Relationship between Health and Social Services: Session 1998-99*, London: The Stationery Office

Department of Health (2000) *The NHS Plan: A Plan for Investment, A Plan for Reform*, London: The Stationery Office

Department of Health (2001a) *National Service Framework for Older People*, London: Department of Health

Department of Health (2001b) *Valuing People: A New Strategy for Learning Disability for the 21st Century*, London: The Stationery Office

Department of Health (2002) *Keys to Partnership: Working Together to Make a Difference in People's Lives*, London: Department of Health

Department of Health (2006) *Our Health, Our Care, Our Say*, London: Department of Health

Department of Health and Social Security (1988) *Community Care: An Agenda for Action*, London: Department of Health

Dickinson, H. (2006) 'The evaluation of health and social care partnerships: an analysis of approaches and synthesis for the future', *Health and Social Care in the Community*, Vol. 14, No. 5, pp. 375–83

Dornan, B. (1999) 'Teamwork in integrated primary health and social care teams', unpublished report, Down Lisburn Trust

Dowling, B., Powell, M. and Glendinning, C. (2004) 'Conceptualising successful partnerships', *Health and Social Care in the Community*, Vol. 12, No. 4, pp. 309–17

El Ansari, W., Phillips, C. and Hammick, M. (2001) 'Collaboration and partnership: developing the evidence base', *Health and Social Care in the Community*, Vol. 9, No. 4, pp. 215–27

Ellis, K., Davis, A, and Rummery, K. (1999) 'Needs assessment, street-level bureaucracy and the new community care', *Social Policy and Administration*, Vol. 33, No. 3, pp. 262–80

Ferguson, I. (2003) 'Social work and social care in the "new" Scotland', in Mooney, G. and Scott, G. (eds) (2003) *Exploring Social Policy in the "New" Scotland*, Bristol: The Policy Press

Glasby, J. (2003) 'Bringing down the "Berlin Wall": the health and social care divide', *British Journal of Social Work*, Vol. 33, No. 7, pp. 969–75

Glasby, J. and Peck, E. (eds) (2004) *Care Trusts: Partnership Working in Action*, Oxford: Radcliffe Publishing

Glendinning, C. (2002) 'Partnerships between health and social services: developing a framework for evaluation', *Policy and Politics*, Vol. 30, No. 1, pp. 115–27

Glendinning, C., Clarke, S., Hare, P., Kotchetkova, I., Maddison, J. and Newbronner, L. (2006) *Outcomes-Focused Social Care Services for Older People: Progress and Possibilities*, York: Social Policy Research Unit

Glendinning, C., Dowling, B. and Powell, M. (2005) 'Partnerships between health and social care under "New Labour": smoke without fire? A review of policy and evidence', *Evidence and Policy*, Vol. 1, No. 3, pp. 365–81

Glendinning, C., Hudson, B., Hardy, B. and Young, R. (2004) 'The Health Act 1999 section 31 partnership "flexibilities"', in Glasby, J. and Peck, E. (eds) (2004) *Care Trusts: Partnership Working in Action*, Abingdon: Radcliffe Medical Press

Glendinning, C., Powell, M. and Rummery, K. (2002) (eds) *Partnerships, New Labour and the Governance of Welfare,* Bristol: The Policy Press

Greer, S. (2001) *Divergence and Devolution,* London: The Constitution Unit/The Nuffield Trust

Greig, R. and Poxton, R. (2000) *Partnership Readiness Framework*, London: Institute of

Applied Health and Social Policy, King's College

Halliday, J., Asthana, S. and Richardson, S. (2004) 'Evaluating partnership: the role of formal assessment tools', *Evaluation*, Vol. 10, No. 3, pp. 285–303

Hardy, B., Hudson, B. and Waddington, E. (2000) *What Makes a Good Partnership? A Partnership Assessment Tool*, Leeds: Nuffield Institute for Health/NHS Executive Trent Region

Hiscock, J. and Pearson, M. (1999) 'Looking inwards, looking outwards: dismantling the "Berlin Wall" between health and social services?', *Social Policy and Administration*, Vol. 33, No. 2, pp. 150–63

House of Commons Health Committee (1998) *First Report: The Relationship between Health and Social Services, Vol. 1*, London: The Stationery Office

Hudson, B. (1987) 'Collaboration in social welfare: a framework for analysis', *Policy and Politics*, Vol. 15, No. 3, pp. 175–82

Hubbard, G. and Themessl-Huber, M. (2005) 'Professional perceptions of joint working in primary care and social care services for older people in Scotland', *Journal of Interprofessional Care* Vol. 19, No. 4, pp. 371–85

Hudson, B. (2002) 'Interprofessionality in health and social care: the Achilles' heel of partnership?', *Journal of Interprofessional Care*, Vol. 16, No. 1, pp. 7–17

Hudson, B. (2007) 'What lies ahead for partnership working? Collaborative contexts and policy tensions', *Journal of Integrated Care*, Vol. 15, No. 3, pp. 29–36

Hudson, B. and Hardy, B. (2002) 'What is a "successful" partnership and how can it be measured?', in Glendinning, C., Powell, M. and Rummery, K. (eds) (2002) *Partnerships, New Labour and the Governance of Welfare*, Bristol: The Policy Press

Hudson, B. and Henwood, M. (2002) 'The NHS and social care: the final countdown?', *Policy and Politics*, Vol. 30, No. 2, pp. 153–66

Hudson, B., Hardy, B., Henwood, M. and Wistow, G. (1997) 'Working across professional boundaries: primary health care and social care', *Public Money and Management*, October–December, pp. 25–30

Infusion Co-operative (2005) *Development of Tools to Measure Service User and Carer Satisfaction with Single Shared Assessment*, Edinburgh: Scottish Executive Social Research

Joint Improvement Team (2006) *Connecting Partnerships: A Framework for Supporting Leadership, Effective Management and Service Innovations across Health and Social Care Partnerships*, Edinburgh: Joint Improvement Team

Kohls, M. (1989) *Stop... Start... Stutter*, Edinburgh: Care in the Community Scottish Working Group

Lewis, J. (2001) 'Older people and the health-social care boundary in the UK: half a century of hidden policy conflict', *Social Policy and Administration*, Vol. 35, No. 4, pp. 343–59

Leutz, W. (1999) 'Five laws for integrating medical and social care: lessons from the US and UK', *The Milbank Memorial Fund Quarterly*, Vol. 77, No. 1, pp. 77–110

Leutz, W. (2005) 'Reflections on integrating medical and social care: five laws revisited', *Journal of Integrated Care*, Vol. 13, No. 5, pp. 3–12

Liddle, A. M. and Gelsthorpe, L. (1994) *Crime Prevention and Inter-agency Co-operation*, Police Research Group Crime Prevention Unit Series: Paper No 53, London: Home Office Police Department

Ling, T. (2000) 'Unpacking partnership: the case of health care', in Clarke, J., Gewirtz, S. and McLaughlin, E. (eds) *New Managerialism, New Welfare?* London: Sage

Mackintosh, M. (1992) 'Partnerships: issues of policy and negotiation', *Local Economy*, Vol. 7, No. 3, pp. 210–24

McWalter, G., Toner, H., Corser, A., Eastwood, J., Marshall, M. and Turvey, T. (1994) 'Needs and needs assessment: their components and definitions with reference to dementia', *Health and Social Care in the Community*, Vol. 2, No. 4, pp. 213–19

Miller, C. and Ahmad, Y. (2000) 'Collaboration and partnership: an effective response to complexity and fragmentation or solution built on sand?', *International Journal of Sociology and Social Policy*, Vol. 20, No. 5-6, pp. 1–38

Molyneaux, J. (2001) 'Interprofessional teamworking: what makes teams work well', *Journal of Interprofessional Care*, Vol. 15, No. 1, pp. 29–35

Mooney, G. and Scott, G. (2005) *Exploring Social Policy in the 'New' Scotland*, Bristol: The Policy Press

Newman, J. (2001) *Modernising Governance*, London: Sage

Nolan, M. and Caldock, K.(1996) 'Assessment: identifying the barriers to good practice', *Health and Social Care in the Community*, Vol. 4, No. 2, pp. 77–85

Ovretveit, J., Mathias, P. and Thompson, T. (1997) *Interprofessional Working for Health and Social Care*, London: Macmillan

Peck, E., Gulliver, P. and Towell, D. (2002) 'Governance of partnership between health and social services: the experience of Somerset', *Health and Social Care in the Community* Vol. 10, No. 5, pp. 331–38

Peck, E., Towell, D. and Gulliver, P. (2001) 'The meanings of "culture" in health and social care: a case study of the combined Trust in Somerset', *Journal of Interprofessional Care*, Vol. 15, No. 4, pp. 319–27

Petch, A. (2003) 'Intermediate care or integrated care: the Scottish perspective on support provision for older people', *Journal of Integrated Care*, Vol. 11, No. 6, pp. 7–14

Petch, A., Cheetham, J., Fuller, R., MacDonald, C., Myers, F. with Hallam, A. and Knapp, M. (1996) *Delivering Community Care: Initial Implementation of Care Management in Scotland*, Edinburgh: HMSO

Petch, A., Miller, E. and Cook, A. (2005) 'Focusing on outcomes: their role in partnership policy and practice', *Journal of Integrated Care*, Vol. 13, No. 6, pp. 3–12

Petch, A., Cook, A., Miller, E., Alexander, H., Cooper, S.-A., Hubbard, G. and Morrison, J. (2007) 'Users and carers define effective partnerships in health and social care'. Available from URL: www.masc.bham.ac.uk/Reports/UCDEP.pdf (accessed 27 September 2007)

Phelps, K. and Regen, E. (2007) 'To what extent does the use of Health Act flexibilities promote effective partnership working and positive outcomes for frail older people?'. Available from URL: www.masc.bham.ac.uk/Reports/HAF.pdf (accessed 27 September 2007)

Pietroni, P. (1996) 'Stereotypes or archetypes? A study of perceptions amongst health care students', in Pietroni, P. and Pietroni, C. (eds) (1996) *Innovation in Community Care and Primary Health: The Marylebone Experiment*, London: Churchill Livingstone

Poxton, R. (1999) *Partnerships in Primary and Social Care*, London: King's Fund

Poxton, R. (2004) 'What makes effective partnerships between health and social care?' in Glasby, J. and Peck, E, (eds) (2004) *Care Trusts: Partnership Working in Action*, Abingdon: Radcliffe Medical Press

Qureshi, H. (ed) (2001) *Outcomes in Social Care Practice*, Outcomes of Community Care Practice 7. York: Social Policy Research Unit

Rummery, K. (2003) 'Progress towards partnership? The development of relations between primary care organisations and social services concerning older people's services in the UK', *Social Policy and Society*, Vol. 3, No. 1, pp. 33–42

Rummery, K. and Coleman, A. (2003) 'Primary health and social care services in the UK: progress towards partnership?' *Social Sciences and Medicine*, Vol. 56, No. 8 pp. 1773–82

Sainsbury Centre for Mental Health (1997) *Effective Partnerships: Developing Key Indicators for Joint Working in Mental Health*, London: Sainsbury Centre for Mental Health

Scottish Executive (1999) *A Scotland where Everyone Matters: Our visions for Social Justice*, Edinburgh: Scottish Executive

Scottish Executive (2000a) *Our National Health: A Plan for Action, a Plan for Change*, Edinburgh: Scottish Executive

Scottish Executive (2000b) *Community Care: A Joint Future*, Edinburgh: Scottish Executive

Scottish Executive (2000c) *The Same as You?*, Edinburgh: Scottish Executive

Scottish Executive (2000d) *Better Government for Older People: All Our Futures in Scotland – Statement on Older People*, Edinburgh: Scottish Executive

Scottish Executive (2000e) *Response to the Royal Commission on Long Term Care*, Edinburgh: Scottish Executive

Scottish Executive (2001a) *Scottish Executive's Response to the Report of the Joint Future Group*, Edinburgh: Scottish Executive

Scottish Executive (2001b) *Better Care for All Our Futures*, Edinburgh: Scottish Executive

Scottish Executive (2002) *Report on the Development of a Resource Use Measure (RUM) for Scotland*, Edinburgh: Scottish Executive

Scottish Executive (2002) *Report of the Integrated Human Resource Working Group on the Human Resource Implications of the Joint Future Agenda*, Edinburgh: Scottish Executive

Scottish Executive (2003a) *Equipped for Inclusion – Report of the Strategy Forum: Equipment and Adaptations*, Edinburgh: Scottish Executive

Scottish Executive (2003b) *Partnership for Care: Scotland's Health White Paper*, Edinburgh: Scottish Executive

Scottish Executive (2003c) *Modernising Government Fund Round 1: Final Report*, Edinburgh: Scottish Executive

Scottish Executive (2003d) *Joint Future Agenda – Short Life Working Group on Joint Premises Development in Primary and Community Care: Final Report*, Edinburgh: Scottish Executive

Scottish Executive (2003e) *Using the Law to Develop and Improve Equipment and Adaptation Provision*, Edinburgh: Scottish Executive, Strategy Forum on Equipment and Adaptations

Scottish Executive (2004) *Better Outcomes for Older People: Draft for Consultation*, Edinburgh: Scottish Executive

Scottish Office (1997a) *Designed to Care: Renewing the National Health Service in Scotland*, Edinburgh: The Stationery Office

Scottish Office (1997b) *A Framework for Mental Health Services in Scotland*, Edinburgh: The Stationery Office

Scottish Office (1998) *Modernising Community Care: An Action Plan,* The Stationery Office

Scottish Parliament (2000) *Inquiry into the Delivery of Community Care*, 16th report of the Health and Community Care Committee 2000, Edinburgh: Scottish Parliament

Stalker, K., Malloch, M., Barry, M. and Watson, J. (2007) *Evaluation of the Implementation of Local Area Co-ordination in Scotland*, Edinburgh: Information and Analytical Services Division, Scottish Executive Education Department

Stewart, A., Petch, A. and Curtice, L. (2003) 'Towards integrated working across health and social care in Scotland: from maze to matrix', *Journal of Interprofessional Care*, Vol. 17, No. 4, pp. 335–50

Stewart, J. (2004) *Taking Stock: Scottish Social Welfare after Devolution*, Bristol: The Policy Press

Sullivan, H., Barnes, M. and Matka, E. (2002) 'Building collaborative capacity through "theories of change"', *Evaluation*, Vol. 8, No. 2, pp. 205–26

Thomas, P. and Palfrey, C. (1996) 'Evaluation: stakeholder-focused criteria', *Social Policy and Administration*, Vol. 30, No. 2, pp. 125–42

Tucker, C. and Brown, L. (1997) *Moving towards the Integration of Health and Social Care: An Evaluation of Different Models for Accessing Community Care Services for Adults and their Carers*, Wiltshire County Council/University of Bath

Villeneau, L., Hill, R., Hancock, M. and Wolf, J. (2001) 'Establishing process indicators for joint working in mental health: rationale and results from a national survey', *Journal of Interprofessional Care*, Vol. 15, No. 4, pp. 329–40

Wyatt, M. (2002) 'Partnerships in health and social care: the implications of government guidance in the 1990s in England, with particular reference to voluntary organisations', *Policy and Politics*, Vol. 30, No. 2, pp. 167–82

Appendix

Matrix of Drivers and Barriers to Integrated Working

Source: Stewart, Petch and Curtice, 2003

NATIONAL POLICY FRAMEWORKS	
Drivers	**Barriers**
comprehensive and integrated	piecemeal and contradictory
encourage strategic approach	promote 'projectitis'
legal, financial and guidance frameworks facilitate	legal, financial and guidance frameworks inhibit
realistic timetables	unrealistic timescales/change agenda
some non-negotiables	anything goes
establish accountability for user-focused outcomes	no national pressure to demonstrate user benefits

LOCAL PLANNING CONTEXT	
Drivers	**Barriers**
planning and decision cycles mesh	incompatible planning and decision cycles
all stakeholders involved from the beginning, unions, operational staff, users and carers	partial/tokenistic involvement of stakeholders
joint acceptance of unmet need	not needs led
agreed, comprehensive vision, owned at all levels	issues seen in isolation, priorities not agreed, based on lowest common denominator
user outcome driven	driven by vested interests
evidence based	a paper strategy
runs with 'good enough' plan, 'leap of faith'	waits for the perfect plan
use of budgets reflects strategic priorities	'spend this money NOW'
some stability	constant restructuring
shared location	dispersed locations
small can be good — knowing the people (but no alternatives)	complexity a barrier (but can be an incentive too)
builds on existing good working relationships, 'success breeds success'	no track record of successful collaboration, 'it has never worked here'
restricted resources induce innovation – need to share, 'less means more', Dunkirk spirit	resources induce complacency — rest on laurels, 'more of the same'
pressure to innovate/change to meet need, 'we can't do it alone' 'necessity is the mother of invention'	no incentives to change, 'it won't work here', 'it won't work now'
sense of momentum – 'the time is now'	baggage of the past

OPERATIONAL FACTORS	
Relations between partners	
Drivers	**Barriers**
partnership model	fragmentation of market
balance of power	power imbalance, strong empires, personal sovereignty
task complex, cannot be achieved by single agency	task simple, no perceived need for outside help
integrated or networked e.g. a new community care organisation OR working as if one agency	islands
accountability agreed/shared	accountability disputed/separate
trust between agencies — permits risk taking	lack of trust — prevents risk taking
pooled resources	different budgets/funding streams
partners share information and skills for the bigger picture	partners have energy only for own agenda
open, honest, transparent communication	defensive, limited communication
shared records/systems — creative use of IT	information not shared — IT an excuse
understands other's limitations	no allowances
respects identities of other agencies	'if only they did it our way!'
integrated working embedded in policies and structures at all levels	integrated working depends only on personal links
informed by knowledge across settings e.g. through joint posts and well selected managers	imbalanced by one agency's or profession's priorities
harmonisation of practice to serve local community	policies, boundaries and catchments not co-terminous

OPERATIONAL FACTORS	
Organisational culture	
Drivers	**Barriers**
perceived interdependence	isolationist
willing to share/adopt good practice	competitive
it is everybody's agenda including accountants, administrators	the professionals' business only
'can do' culture	sees institutional and legal barriers
organic, flexible, more autonomy/ delegated responsibility e.g. devolved budgets	rigid, high bureaucratic controls, 'everything has to be checked'
across boundary work WITHIN agencies	departmentalism, preciousness
values difference	values uniformity
collective responsibility publicly demonstrated	senior figures devalue/disown common purpose

OPERATIONAL FACTORS	
Change management	
Drivers	**Barriers**
task focused	bogged down in resolving organisational problems
service managed as a system to reduce confusion	complexity
commitment and flexibility to solve ongoing problems	hides behind legal barriers
rewards success, carrots and sticks	blames, only sticks
willing to devolve responsibility to joint service managers	confuses accountability with direct responsibility for spending
dedicated resources for development, margin for change and innovation	resources too tight, fully committed to existing buildings/staff/ways of working
commits development resources to engineer system change	notches up new projects, mainstream services unaffected
promoted by management at critical stages	stifled/undermined by management
process driven by individuals with leadership qualities and enthusiasm/ managers with knowledge of different settings	no champions
flexible enough to learn as goes, listens/ evaluates, honest about what works	presses on regardless
sustains and rolls out good practice	when champions leave, innovation dies

OPERATIONAL FACTORS	
Enabling staff	
Drivers	**Barriers**
supports champions who work across boundaries	supports those who maintain empires
invests in ownership by staff and users	a management issue
clarity of purpose transmitted to staff and users	'more paperwork! more procedures!', 'what is the purpose of all this?'
enables innovation to come through	stifles the creativity of others
clear co-ordination mechanism	nobody's responsibility
clear written protocols, confidentiality concerns addressed	'no map, I will have to consult my line manager'
clarification of remits, agreed roles and procedures e.g. joint protocols, team structures	unclear responsibilities, conflict
efforts made to reduce complexity	staff left to resolve variation
time to develop and service integrated working — and have joint training, team building	rush in, staff too pressured to collaborate or prepare
collaboration and negotiation valued and part of training	'another meeting – I suppose you were networking again!'
training available for new skills	'I feel de-skilled by these changes'

OPERATIONAL FACTORS	
Professional behaviour	
Drivers	**Barriers**
willing to change	burnt out
centred on user need	tribal, protectionist, different terms and conditions
confident and flexible	threatened and restrictive
accept challenges to mindset and learns	retreats when challenged
willing to take risks	covers own back

OPERATIONAL FACTORS	
Attitudes	
Drivers	**Barriers**
'we have nothing to lose', 'we have everything to gain'	'we have everything to lose', 'we have nothing to gain'
'stolen with pride'	'not invented here!'
'that's a great idea'	'not as interesting as my pet project', 'not a model we recognise', 'doesn't fit our procedures'
'we all own this'	'WE own this'
'I am confident in my skills – though I have more to learn and I respect your skills'	'I'm not sure what I know and I'm threatened by what you know', 'this is my turf'
'we will find a way'	hide behind legal barriers, 'no way'

OPERATIONAL FACTORS	
Outcomes	
Drivers	**Barriers**
user focused and defined outcomes	outcomes only seen from agencies' agenda
visible outcomes	invisible outcomes
benefits shared	winners and losers
some short-term gains	only long-term gains

Index